Critical Thinking for Grade 2 and 3

(Supplemental workbook for CogAT®, OLSAT® and NNAT® and GATE® Testing)

Authored by Bright Minds Publishing

Copyright© by Bright Minds Publishing. All the questions have been prepared by staff at Bright Minds Publishing.

CogAT® is a registered *trademark* of Houghton Mifflin Harcourt™. *OLSAT*® and NNAT2®/NNAT3® are registered *trademarks* of Pearson Education™.

Houghton Mifflin Harcourt, Pearson Education was not involved in authoring this book in any way. This is not an official or certified guide to the CogAT, OLSAT and NNAT test material.

No part of this book may be distributed, photocopied or edited without written consent from the author.

Bright Minds Publishing

Contents

Critical Thinking for Grade 2 and Grade 3   Bright Minds Publishing

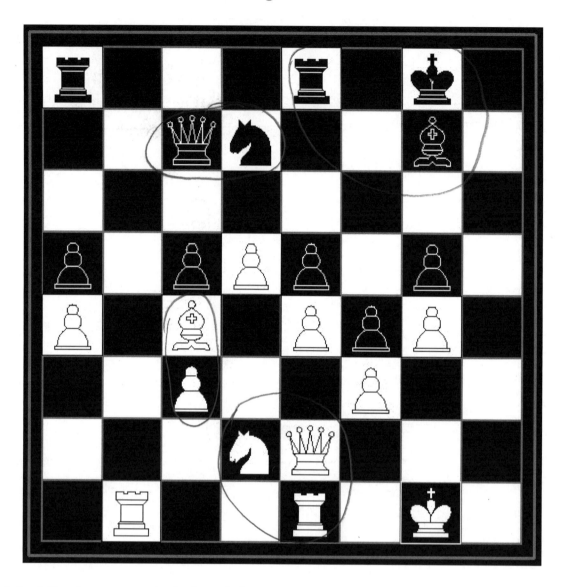

Find the following patterns in the board above

 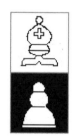  

The given group of words if written as the correct rows, show up again in the columns! E.g. the three words – AGE, CAP and PEG – placed in rows 1, 2, 3 respectively, appear in columns 1, 2, 3 again!

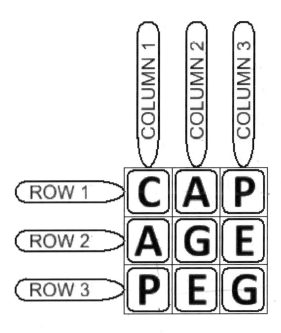

Can you arrange the words given on the next page, in the correct rows of the grids so that the words appear again in the columns too?

EEL, ALE, PEA	TEN, ONE, GOT

TEA, HAT, ATE	GEM, BIG, ICE

CAR, ERA, ACE	EYE, LEG, GEL

AREA, CART, REAP, TAPE	IDEA, DIME, MESS, EASY

Complete the triangular array of numbers below, such that each number is the sum of the two numbers above it, as shown in the examples

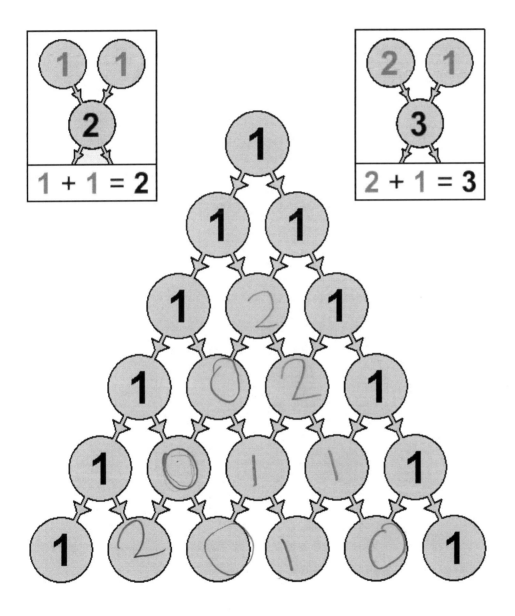

Inspect the following words and the image of the same:

Math is fun!

Following are images of some words - what do the words say:

 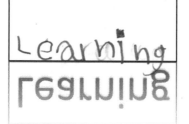 

A frog on a pogo stick starts from stone number 1 and skips every other stone as he moves along a paved path. Would he step on the following stones?

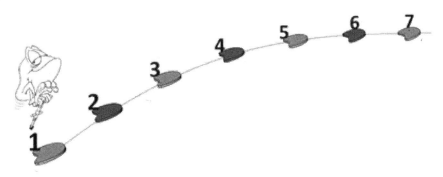

	Yes	No		Yes	No
3	✓	○	64	○	✓
11	✓	○	23	✓	○
32	○	○	49	○	○
54	○	✓	65	✓	○
76	✓	○	88	○	○
97	✓	○	100	○	○

Steven the kangaroo likes to hop from one even number bush to the next. He starts from bush number 2. Will he land on the following bushes?

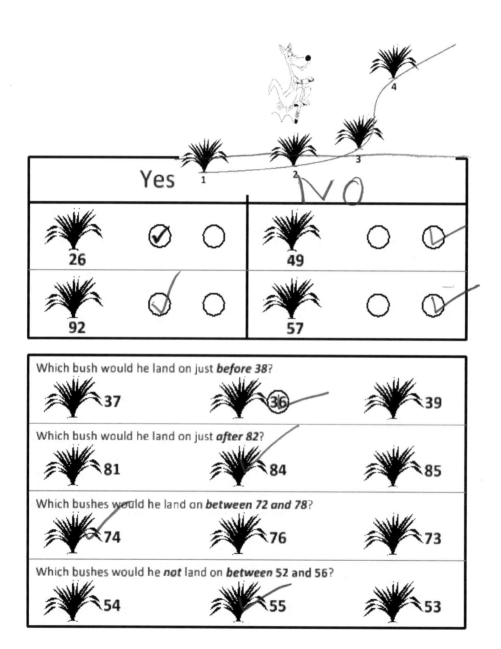

A cloud of numbers is given below, hidden in it are two objects. One can be found by connecting all the odd numbers from 1 to 71, while the other object can be found by connecting all the even numbers from 2 to 90. A point may have two numbers if more than one line passes through it. The start points (numbers 1 and 2) are bold and highlighted with a gray oval.

Hint: Use two different colors for these two objects can make them stand out.

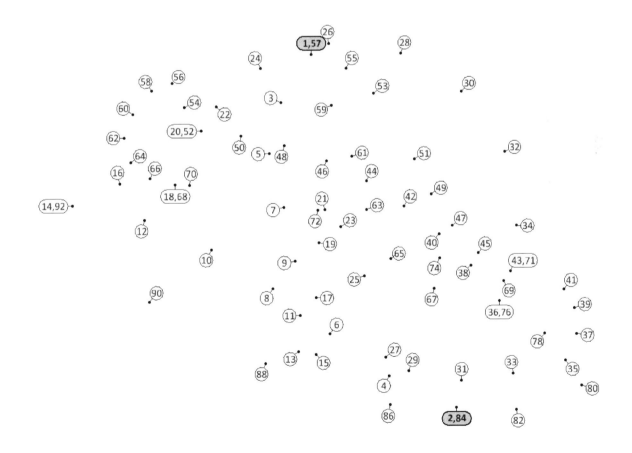

In the cloud of numbers given below, hide two objects – one outlined by odd numbers and the other by the even numbers. Use two different colors to connect them. The points with two numbers are used twice. The start points are highlighted with a gray oval.

Hint: Use two different colors for these two objects can make them stand out.

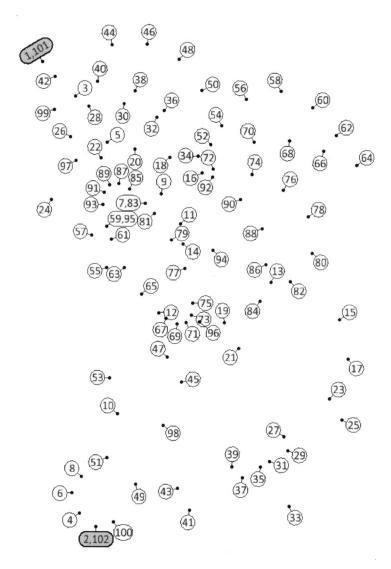

A secret message has reached an army camp, from which only every fifth alphabet is to be read. But the scribe is not able to count by five. Can you help him decode the message?
The first four letters from the message are decoded as shown below.
Remember to count the spaces too!

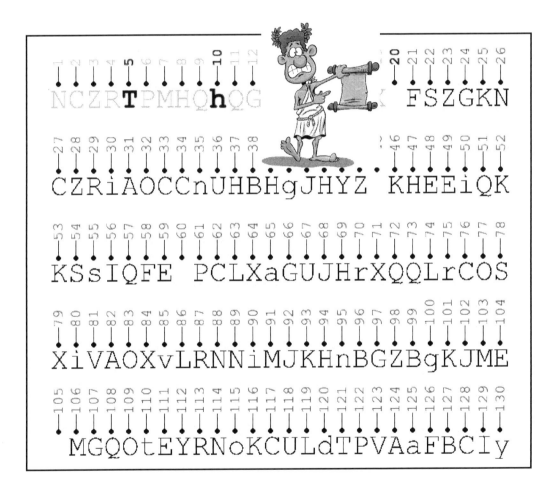

A cookie factory gets their chocolate in the form of individual cubes, bars of ten cubes and sheets of hundred cubes. Each batch of cookies takes a specific number of chocolate cubes. Can you quickly count the number of cubes sent from the pantry below?

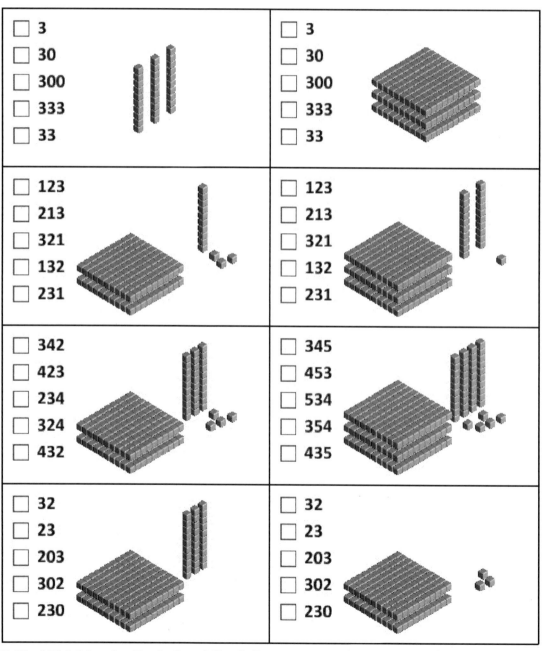

☐ 3	☐ 3
☐ 30	☐ 30
☐ 300	☐ 300
☐ 333	☐ 333
☐ 33	☐ 33

☐ 123	☐ 123
☐ 213	☐ 213
☐ 321	☐ 321
☐ 132	☐ 132
☐ 231	☐ 231

☐ 342	☐ 345
☐ 423	☐ 453
☐ 234	☐ 534
☐ 324	☐ 354
☐ 432	☐ 435

☐ 32	☐ 32
☐ 23	☐ 23
☐ 203	☐ 203
☐ 302	☐ 302
☐ 230	☐ 230

Critical Thinking for Grade 2 and Grade 3   Bright Minds Publishing

Place Values

In the number pairs given in the table below, the same digit appears at different places. With the change in place, its value changes too! Can you find the value of the digit in each case?

What is the value of the digit **3** in the number **138** ☐ **3** ☐ **30** ☐ **300**	What is the value of the digit **3** in the number **381** ☐ **3** ☐ **30** ☐ **300**
What is the value of the digit **1** in the number **138** ☐ **10** ☐ **100** ☐ **1**	What is the value of the digit **1** in the number **381** ☐ **100** ☐ **10** ☐ **1**
What is the value of the digit **8** in the number **138** ☐ **80** ☐ **8** ☐ **800**	What is the value of the digit **8** in the number **381** ☐ **8** ☐ **800** ☐ **80**
What is the value of the digit **0** in the number **750** ☐ **1** ☐ **0** ☐ **100**	What is the value of the digit **0** in the number **705** ☐ **10** ☐ **100** ☐ **0**

Find the Object

Identify the object at a given grid position

Cryptography

The following key is used to encode the words given. Can you decode them?

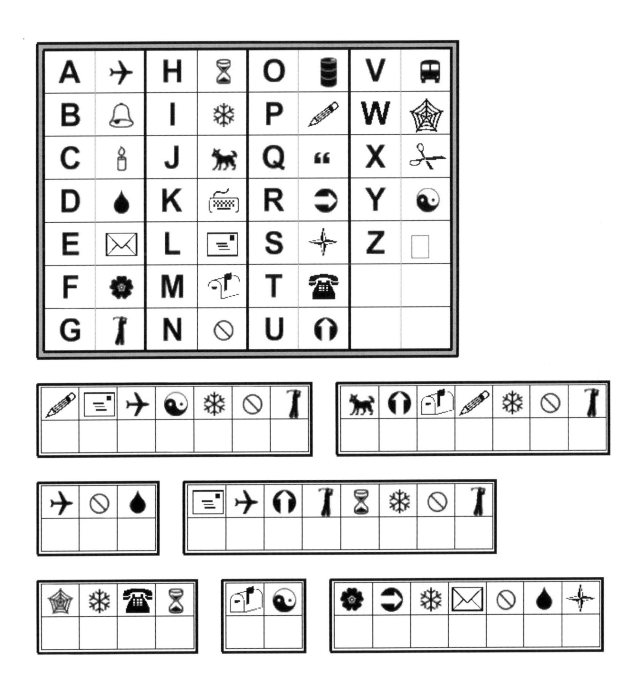

A school nurse's office has several quilts with patchwork showing math sums. Some of the patches are missing.

Can you figure the numbers on these missing patches?

The sums are written both horizontally and vertically as shown below. Remember, the equal to sign (=) says that the quantities on its right and left side are equal.

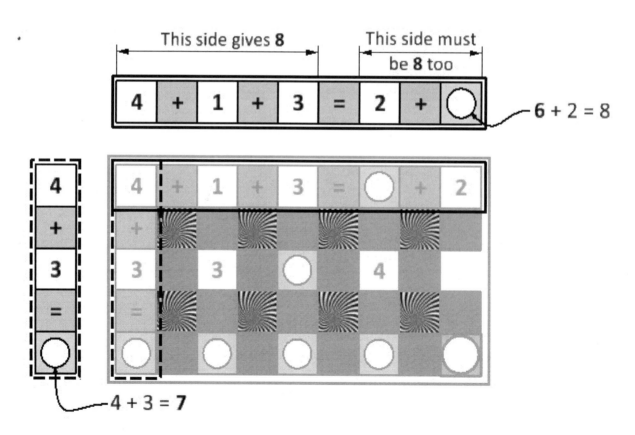

This side gives **8**

This side must be **8** too

$$4 + 1 + 3 = 2 + \bigcirc$$

$6 + 2 = 8$

$4 + 3 = 7$

Number Quilt 1

In the number quilt below, numbers are missing from some of the patches. Can you find those numbers? The sums can be read both horizontally and vertically (top to bottom).

Only the rows or columns with a single missing number can be solved. These are marked with an arrow and you can start by solving these first.

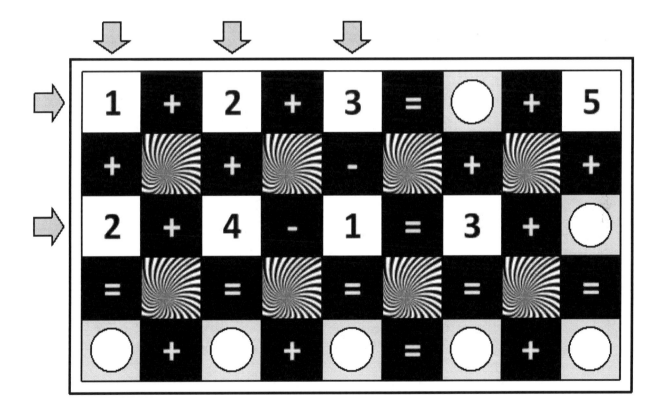

In the number quilt below, numbers are missing from some of the patches. Can you find those numbers? The sums can be read both horizontally and vertically (top to bottom).

Only the rows or columns with a single missing number can be solved. These are marked with an arrow and you can start by solving these first.

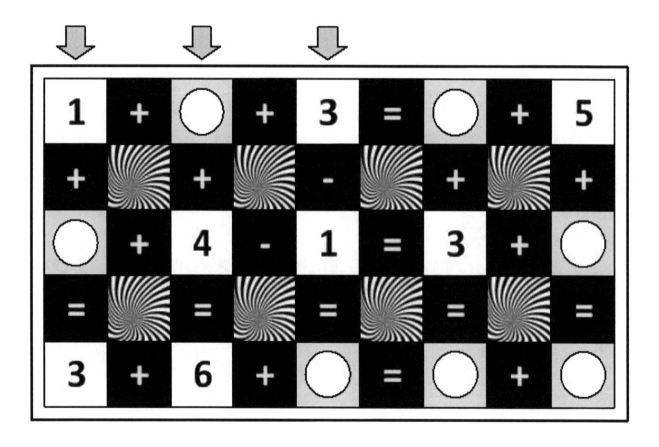

In the number quilt below, numbers are missing from some of the patches. Can you find those numbers? The sums can be read both horizontally and vertically (top to bottom).

Only the rows or columns with a single missing number can be solved. These are marked with an arrow and you can start by solving these first.

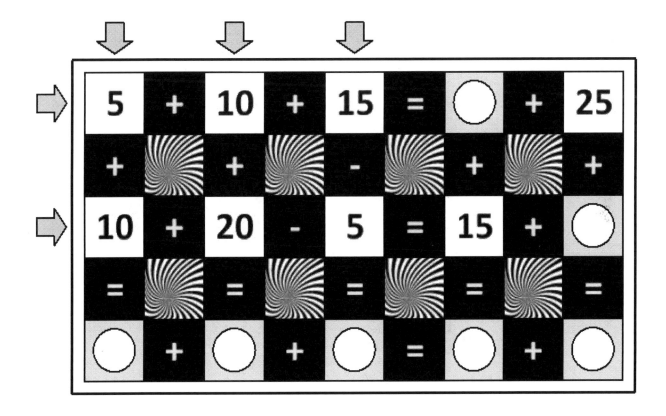

In the number quilt below, numbers are missing from some of the patches. Can you find those numbers? The sums can be read both horizontally and vertically (top to bottom).

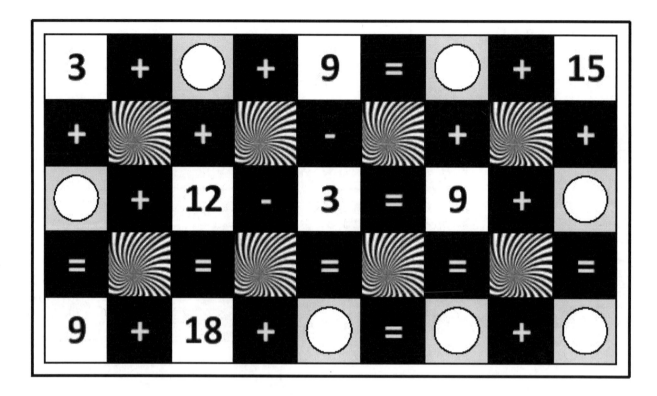

Number Quilt 5

In the number quilt below, numbers are missing from some of the patches. Can you find those numbers? The sums can be read both horizontally and vertically (top to bottom).

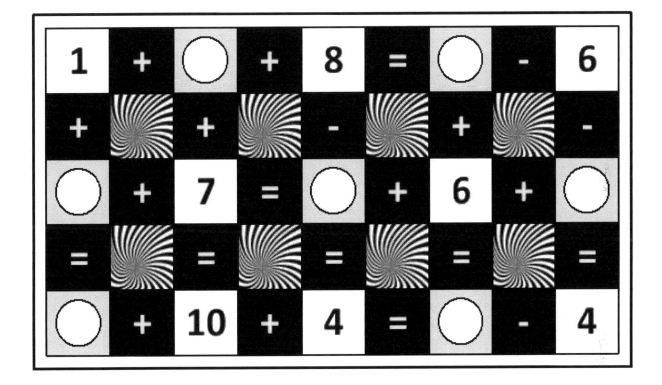

Draw the pattern below in the in the grid and color the various shapes.

Rangoli is an art form practiced in India. It is drawn in homes to celebrate various festivals. You can participate too by drawing the following pattern. Enjoy!

Some of the numbers and alphabets have line of symmetry. Draw the line of symmetry for the ones that have it. Circle the ones that don't have line of symmetry.

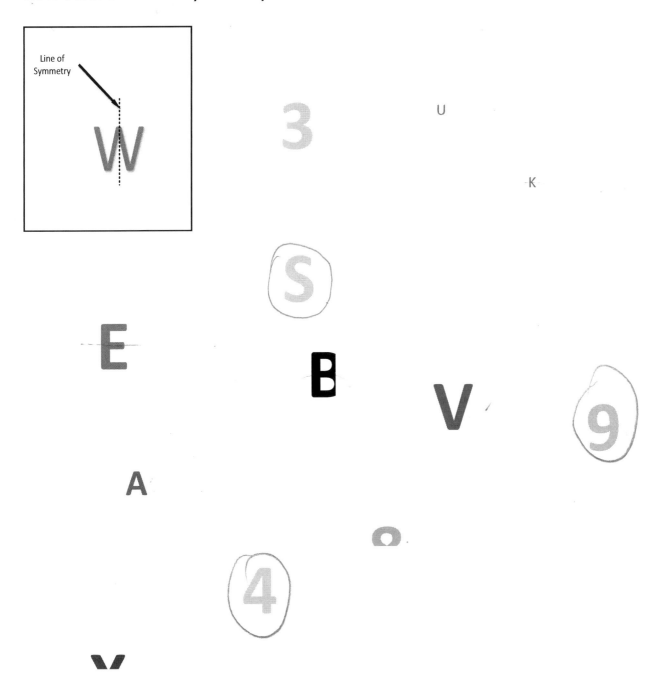

Garbled Proverb

Following sentences are garbled pieces of a proverb. Arrange the words to form a meaningful proverb.

[1] ends that All's well well

Proverb: _____

[2] makes perfect Practice.

Proverb: _____

[3] sure race Slow but the wins.

Proverb: _____

[4] the is policy best Honesty

Proverb: _____

[5] while the shines hay Make sun.

Proverb: _____

[6] before you Look leap

Proverb: _____

[7] indeed A friend friend is a need in

Proverb: _____

[8] the spice is Variety of life

Proverb: _____

[9] bird catches worm early The the

Proverb: _____

[10] Birds feather together of a flock

Proverb: _____

In each of the following figures, find the number of squares of all sizes.

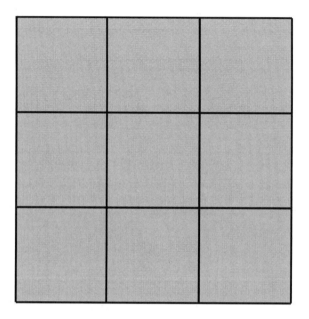

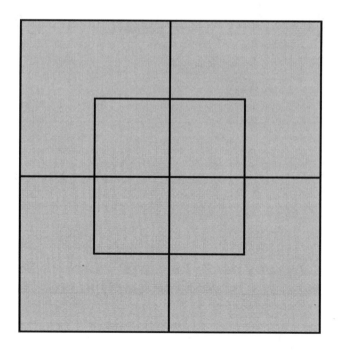

In each of the following figures, find the number of triangles of all sizes.

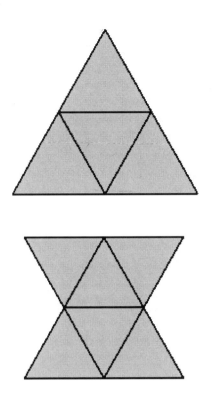

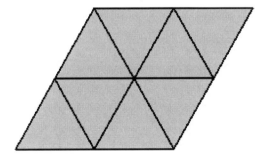

Palindromes are words that read the same way from both directions (example: Mom)

Circle the words that are palindromes

papa

rotor

motor

level

father

mom

civic

da

no

Radar

d

on

Madam

wow

Anagrams

An anagram is a word or phrase that is made by rearranging the letters of another word or phrase. Imagine the original word made from toy blocks or alphabet tiles of scrabble. Then if you can arrange all those toy blocks or tiles into another meaningful word, you have found an anagram!

Lady loves to solve anagrams and Joe loves to solve them too!

Here, the words SOLVE and LOVES use the same letters. They are in fact anagrams!

Six words formed using toy blocks are given below. In each case the blocks can be rearranged to form two other words – the anagrams.

Can you find these anagrams from the six words given below and write them on the blank blocks in each row?

SEAT	FADE	BEAK	LEAF	TUNA	CLAM

Six words formed using toy blocks are given below. In each case the blocks can be rearranged to form two other words – the anagrams.

Can you find these anagrams from the six words given below and write them on the blank blocks in each row?

JETS	COIN	PEEK	HEAR	LEAF	PAGE

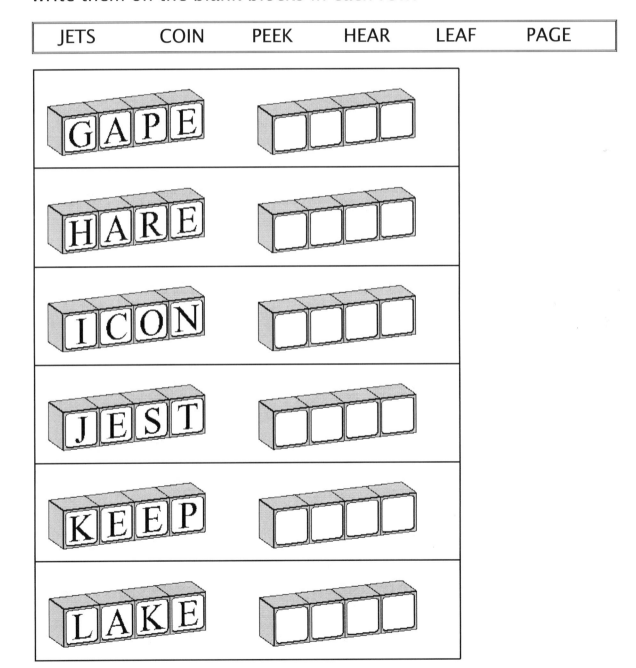

Six words formed using toy blocks are given below. In each case the blocks can be rearranged to form two other words – the anagrams.

Can you find these anagrams from the six words given below and write them on the blank blocks in each row?

| MERIT | STATE | TAPES | TRAPS | VERSE | NAILS |

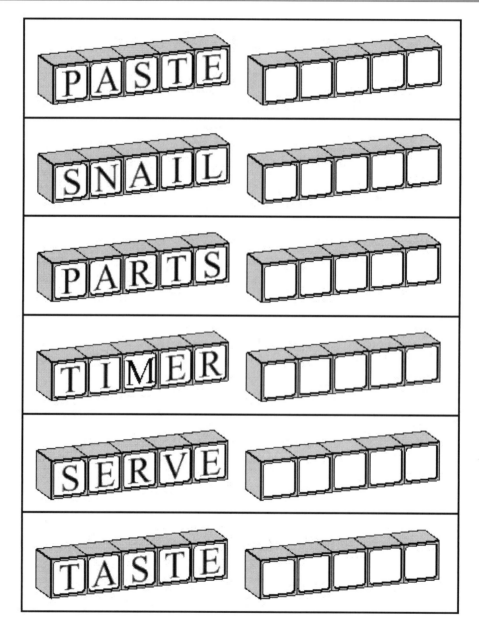

Five words formed using toy blocks are given below. In each case the blocks can be rearranged to form two other words – the anagrams.

Can you find these anagrams from the ten words given below and write them on the blank blocks in each row?

SIREN	PLATE	RESIN	PLEAT	SPOOL
STEER	POOLS	TREES	MILES	SMILE

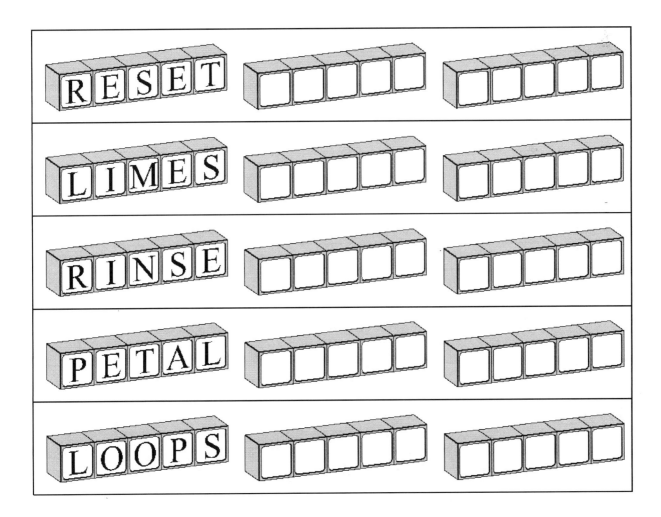

Six words formed using toy blocks are given below. In each case the blocks can be rearranged to form two other words – the anagrams.

Can you find these anagrams from the twelve words given below and write them on the blank blocks in each row?

Square Maze

Show the spaceship a path to the center of the square maze

What if it were a triangular maze? Then our spaceship would have to take sharper turns, which requires slowing down. So what will happen if we have a pentagonal maze?

You guessed it right! We can take the turns much faster!

Let's do that next!

Pentagonal Maze

Show the path for spaceship to the center of this Pentagonal Maze.

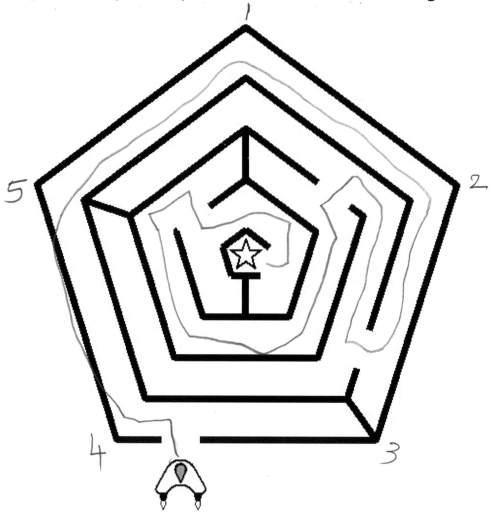

From squares to pentagons now! The number of sides are going a step higher! Pentagons too are closed shapes, but unlike triangles and squares, it is not easy to arrange them without gaps. So we rarely see houses with all pentagonal rooms. But our spaceship should have no problem reaching the heart of this pentagonal maze.

Show the path for spaceship to the center of this Pentagonal Maze.

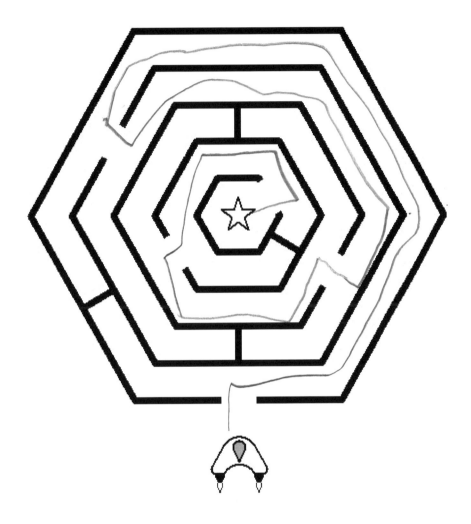

We will keep going from pentagons to hexagons. Here are five of them one inside the other. They are all nicely centered within each other. So our spaceship will have a path that does not suddenly become narrower! Such shapes that share a common center are said to be concentric.

Show the honeybee to the prize at the center of hexagonal hive maze Remove? Have the honeybee go inside and reach her crown. Change the envelope to honeybee

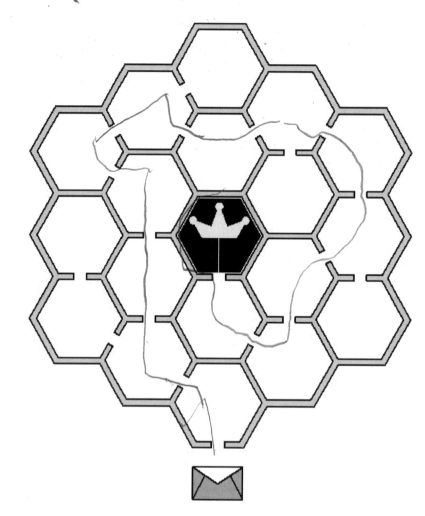

Hexagons can be nicely packed without any gaps. Honey bees do that as they build their hive. What more it takes the less amount of wax to build a hexagonal cell than a square or a triangular cell with as much room! Should we congratulate the queen for her grand design? Here is a card you can help deliver to her.

Can you help the pilot navigate through the storm clouds to the sunny opening at the center?

Reading the road signs is vital for reaching the destination safely. That is where the driver below needs your help!

The weather is cold are foggy and the visibility is poor. The driver is not able to see the signs clearly.

Could you help him?

The starting position is marked on the road. Mark the correct sequence of the road signs as he would see them.

Find the order in which the road signs will be seen on the stretch of road below.

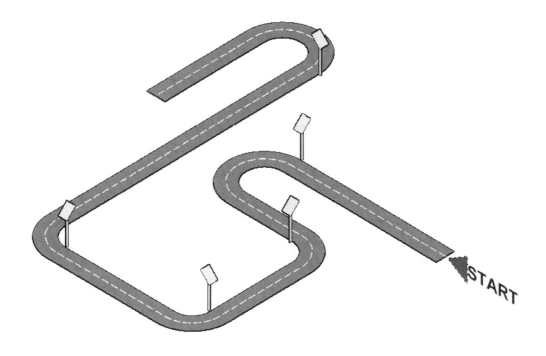

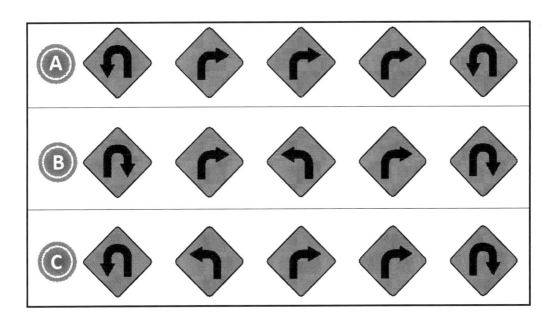

Find the order in which the road signs should be posted on the stretch of road below.

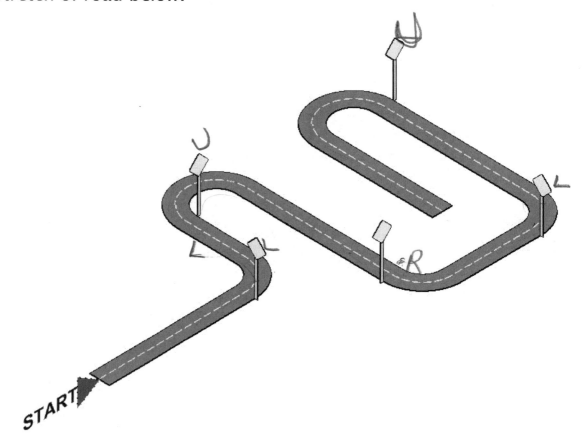

START

Select the sequence of road signs seen during the short drive shown

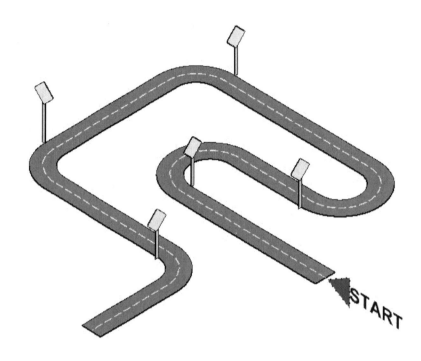

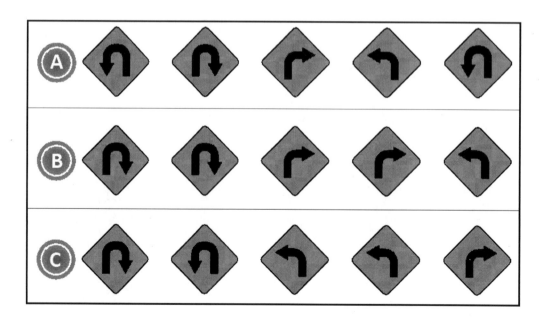

Select the sequence of road signs seen during the short drive shown

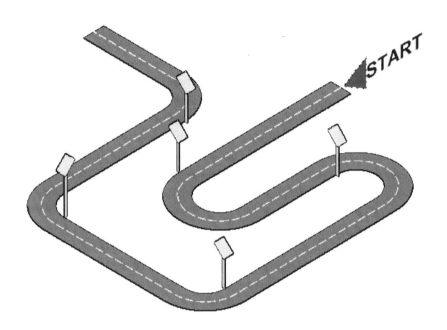

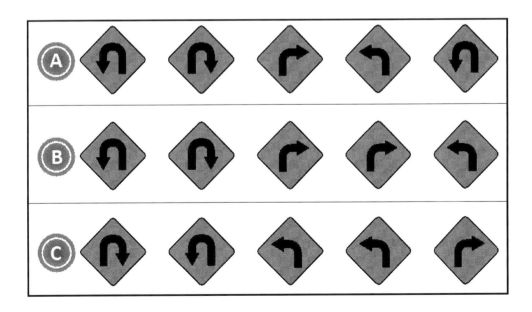

Find the correct sequence of the road signs encountered on the road below.

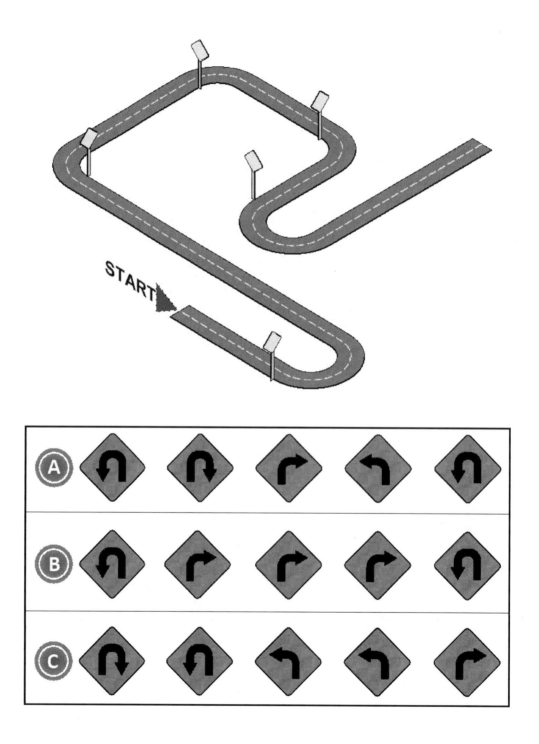

Road Signs #6

Find the correct sequence of the road signs encountered on the road below.

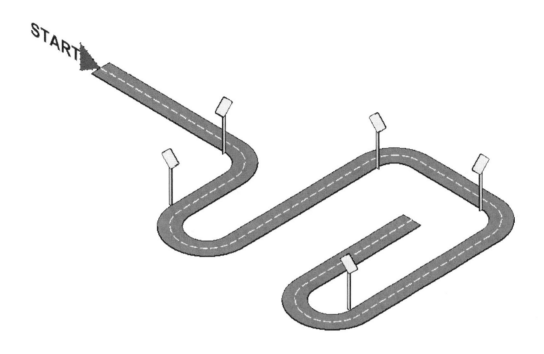

Cubes are like squares. All their sides are equal. But a square is flat or two dimensional, while a cube is a three dimensional solid. Cubes can be neatly stacked in a pile.

Count the cubes stacked together in picture below (remember to count the ones that are hidden behind other cubes)

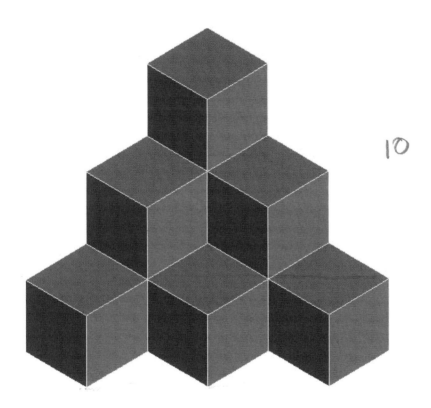

10

Cylinders are like circles, but they have height too. They have two flat faces that help us stack them as shown.

Count the cylinders stacked together in picture below (Remember to count the ones that are hidden behind other cylinders)

Imagine a cylinder that is carved to hold water or even coffee. Now we have a mug or a glass! But they are really cylinders to start with and hence we can stack them too!

Count the mugs stacked together in picture below (Remember to count the ones that are hidden behind other mugs)

Prisms are long solids which have the same shape and thickness everywhere along their length. Here are some hexagonal prisms stacked in piles.

Count the prisms stacked together in picture below (Remember to count the ones that are hidden behind other prisms)

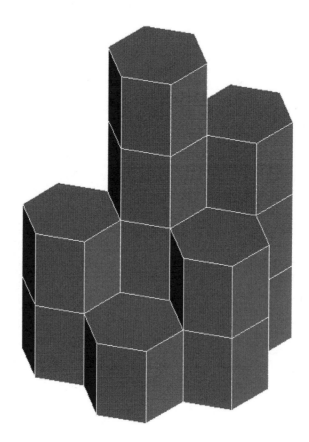

Prisms are long solids which have the same shape and thickness everywhere along their length. Here are some pentagonal prisms stacked in piles.

Count the prisms stacked together in picture below (Remember to count the ones that are hidden behind other prisms)

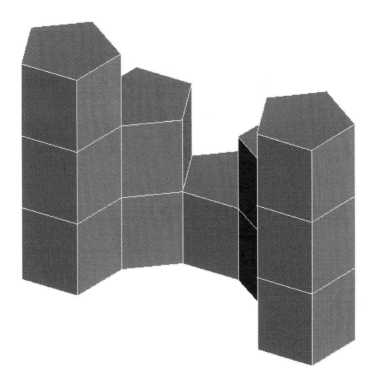

Prisms can be laid on their side too. And then they can be stacked like logs. Here are some triangular prisms stacked in piles.

Count the prisms stacked together in picture below (Remember to count the ones that are hidden behind other prisms)

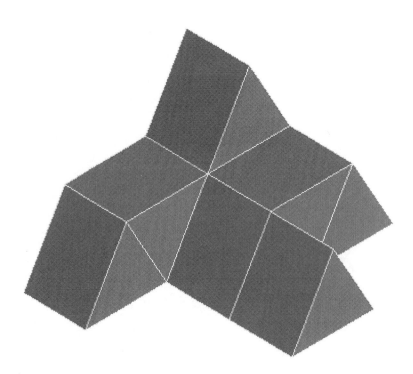

Number Pyramids

The pharaoh has ordered lots of pyramids and the royal architect Pyramedea is busy building them! She has set up a factory to quarry the stone blocks, chisel them to their exact shape and have them transported down the river to reach the building site.

To make sure each stone block gets correctly placed, it is numbered with the sum of the numbers on the two blocks that support it. Four boat have arrived, laden with the blocks. Locate the one that carries all the right ones.

Remember the shape of the blocks matters too!

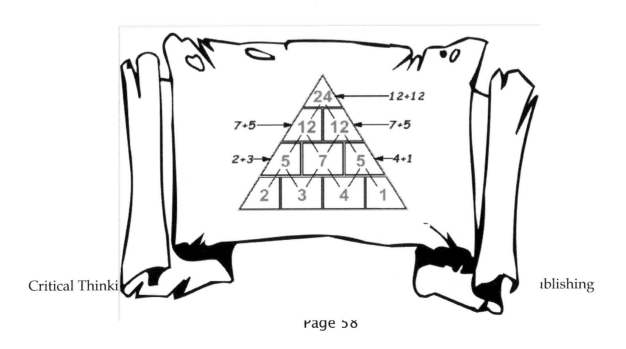

Find which boat is carrying the blocks needed for this pyramid?

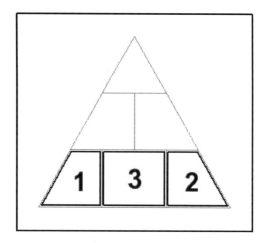

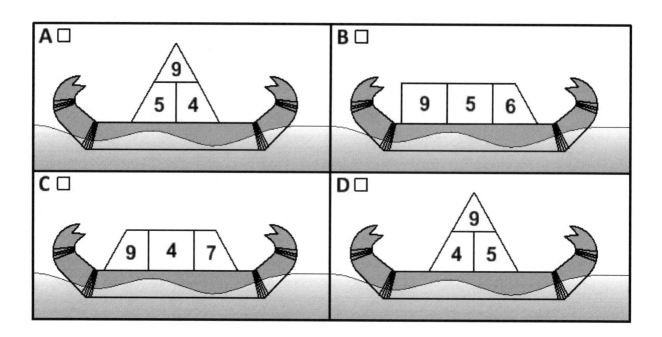

Find which boat is carrying the blocks for this pyramid?

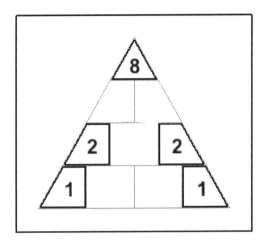

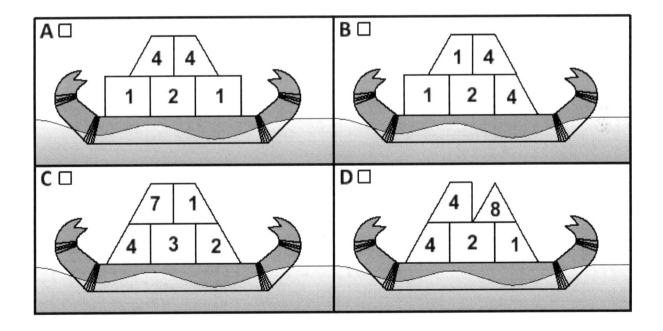

Find which boat is carrying the blocks for this pyramid?

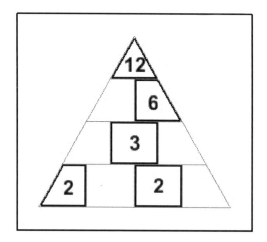

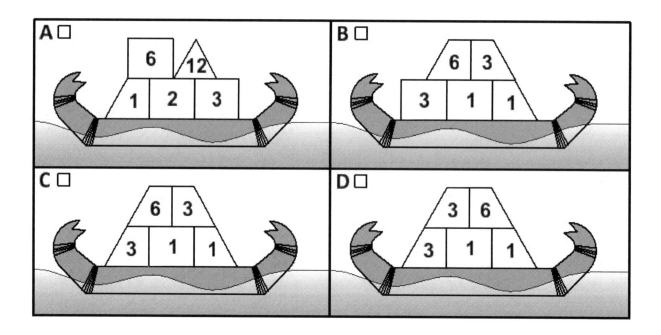

Find which boat is carrying the blocks for this pyramid?

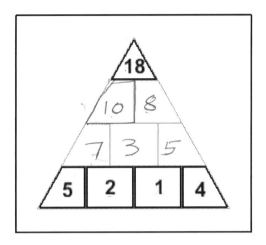

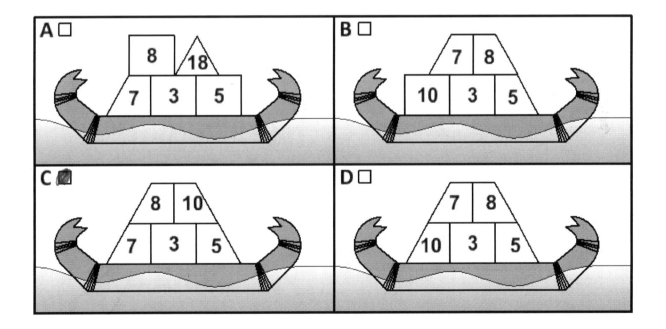

Number Pyramid #5

Number Pyramid #5

Find which boat is carrying the blocks for this pyramid?

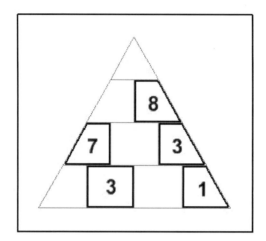

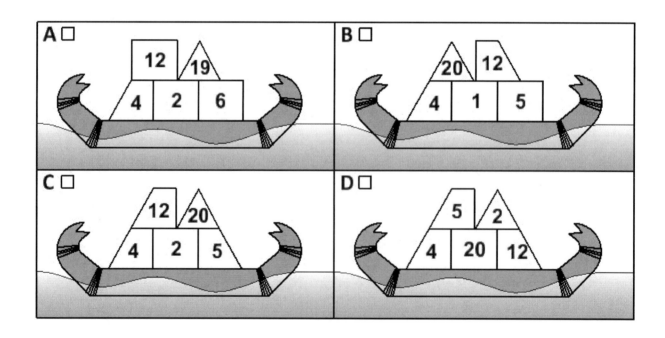

Find which boat is carrying the blocks for this pyramid?

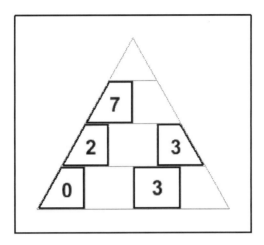

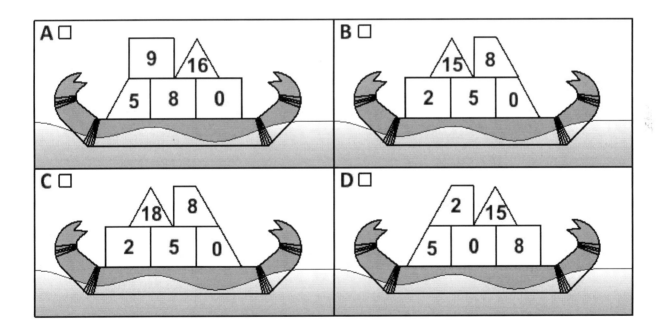

Bricks and cookies have a lot in common. Just as a cookie is made from dough, shaped by a cookie cutter and then baked in an oven; a brick is made from clay, shaped with a mold and then fired in a kiln till it is hard.

Here, we are going to match a mold to a brick that came from it.

Mold   **Brick**

Find which brick came from the mold shown below (remember, you might need to rotate the bricks in your mind to match them with the mold)

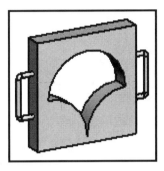

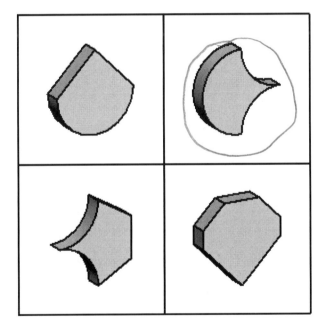

Critical Thinking for Grade 2 and Grade 3 Bright Minds Publishing

Find the brick came from the mold shown below (Remember, you might need to rotate the bricks in your mind to match them with the mold)

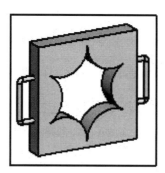

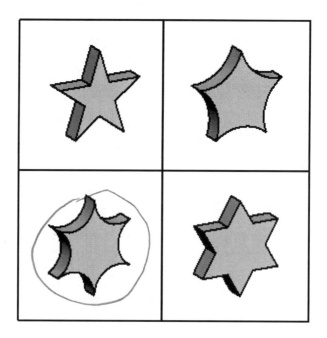

Find the brick that came from the mold shown below (Remember, you might need to rotate the bricks in your mind to match them with the mold)

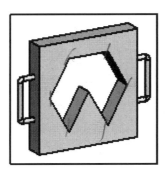

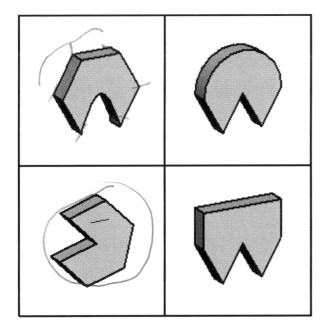

Find the brick that came from the mold shown below (Remember, you might need to rotate the bricks in your mind to match them with the mold)

Bricks and a Mold #5

Find the brick that came from the mold shown below (Remember, you might need to rotate the bricks in your mind to match them with the mold)

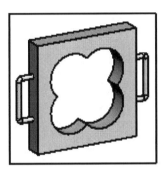

Which of the four bricks came from the mold shown? Remember, you might need to rotate the bricks in your mind to match them with the mold.

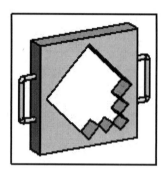

The excavation at an archeological site, uncovers a set of ancient coins. With it is a tablet carrying the king's decree, that no denomination may be repeated in any transaction.

E.g. to make the sum of say 15, only one each of the coins 1, 2, 4 and 8 were allowed as shown below –

1 + 2 + 4 + 8 = 15 Allowed!

1 + 2 + 2 + 2 + 8 = 15 Forbidden! One coin got repeated thrice!

Coin Selection #1

Select the coins to make up the sum shown.

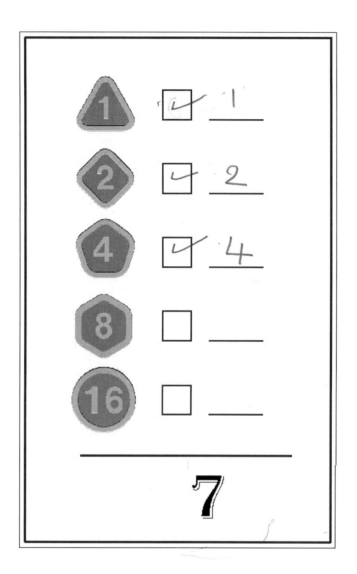

Select the coins to make up the sum shown

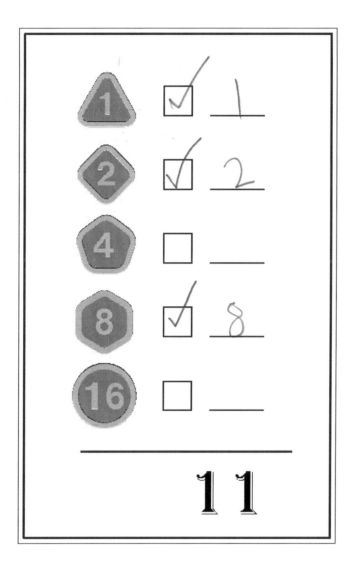

Select the coins to make up the sum shown

Select the coins to make up the sum shown

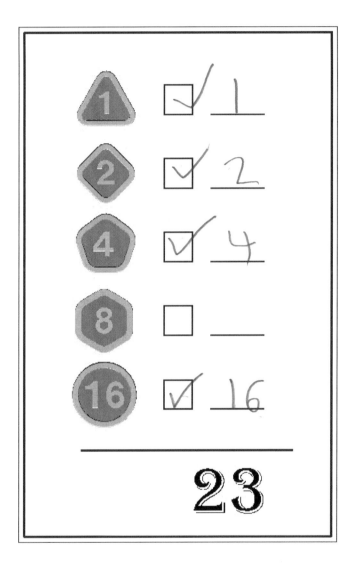

Select the coins to make up the sum shown

Select the coins to make up the sum shown

A tire rolling on the ground has a dab of wet paint, which is leaving stains on the ground as shown. As it rolls further, which numbers would get stained?

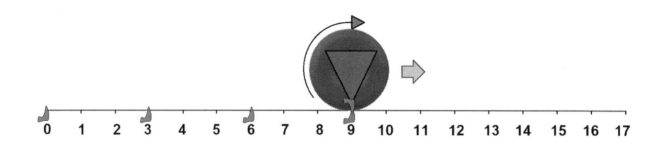

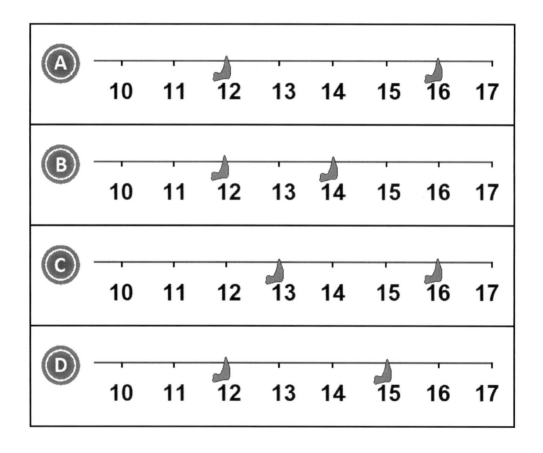

A tire rolling on the ground has a dab of wet paint, which is leaving stains on the ground as shown. As it rolls further, which numbers would get stained?

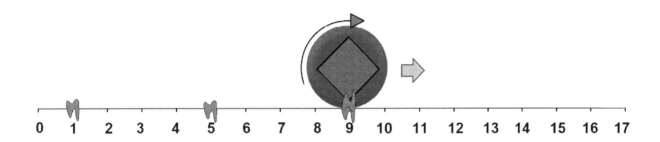

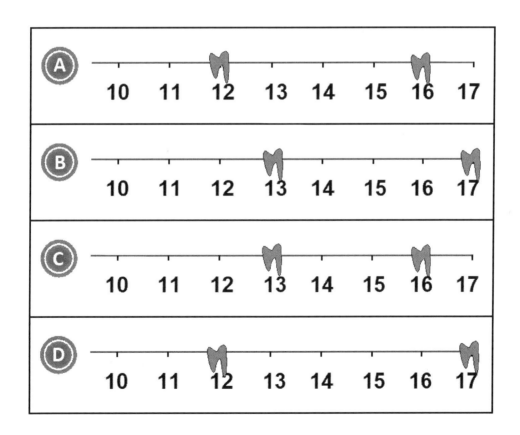

A tire rolling on the ground has a dab of wet paint, which is leaving stains on the ground as shown. As it rolls further, which numbers would get stained?

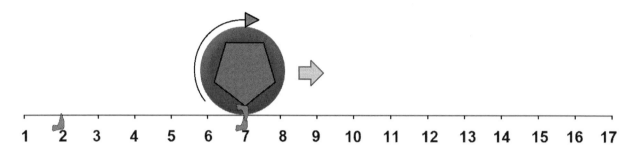

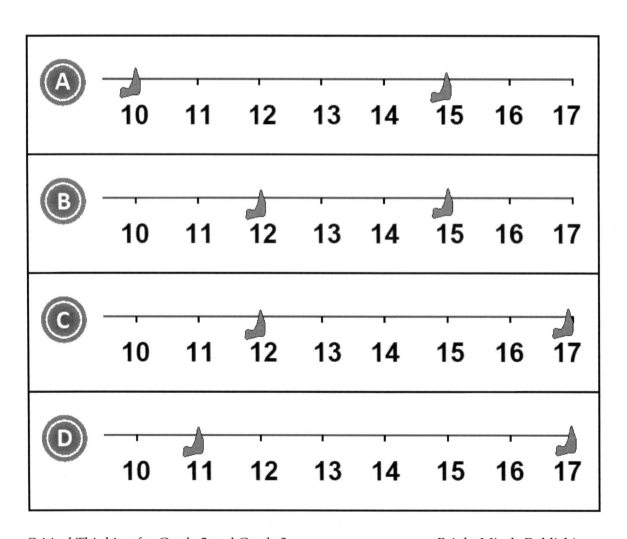

A tire rolling on the ground has some dabs of wet paint, which are leaving stains on the ground as shown. As it rolls further, which numbers would get stained?

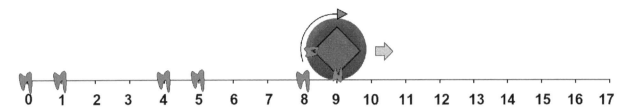

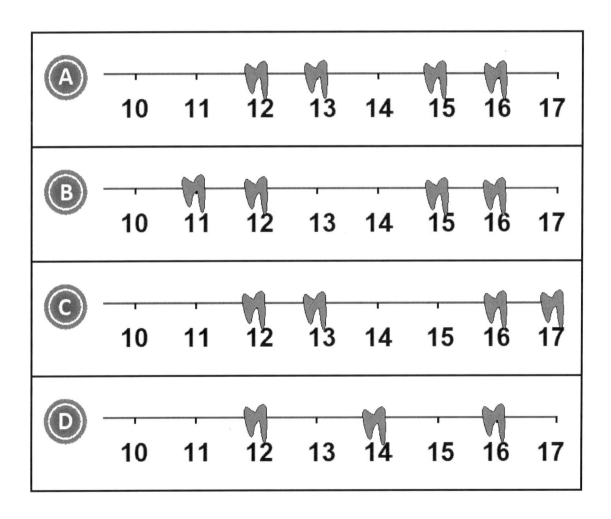

A tire rolling on the ground has gets two dabs of wet paint, which are leaving stains on the ground as shown. As it rolls further, which numbers would get stained?

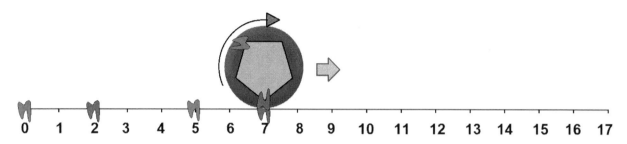

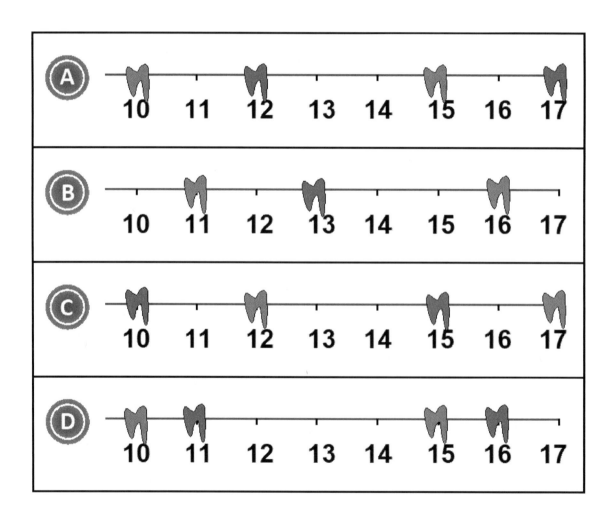

A kangaroo and her joey (baby kangaroo) start leaping together from 0. They both land on the number 10 as shown. What is the next number on which both of them will land?

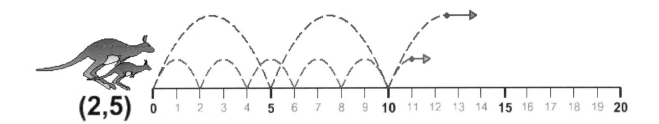

A kangaroo and her joey (baby kangaroo) start leaping together from 0. What is the next number on which both of them will land?

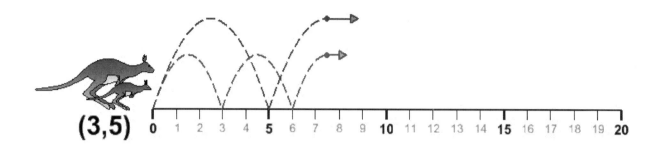

A kangaroo and her joey (baby kangaroo) start leaping together from 0. What is the next number on which both of them will land?

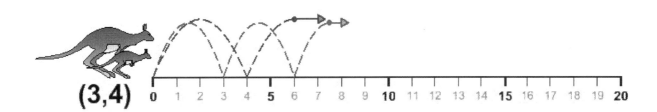

(3,4)

A kangaroo and her joey (baby kangaroo) start leaping together from 0. What is the next number on which both of them will land?

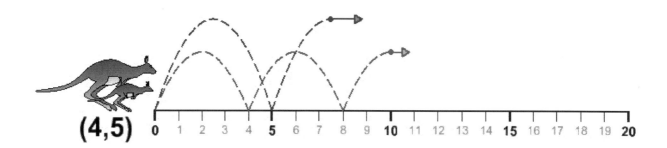

(4,5)

A kangaroo and her joey (baby kangaroo) start leaping together from 0. What is the next number on which both of them will land?

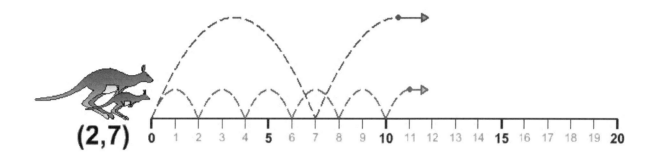

(2,7)

Find matching image

Find the image that matches the image in the 1st square

Create your own code

A = đ	B = ℧	C = Ⅎ	D = 'Ω
E = Γ	F = Δ	G = Π	H = Σ
I = Φ	J = Ђ	K = ϕ	L = ϵ
M = ?	N = ₵	O = Ω	P = Ɛ
Q = Ж	R = Φ̄	S = ◬	T = ⊥̇
U = ∩	V = ∉	W = ∏	X = Σ
Y = ζ	Z = ⊼		

How will you compose the following message?

I love my family

= _____

Now break the following code.

Σđ Πđ Φ Φ   Φ◬ ℧ Γ đ∩⊥̇ Φ Δ ∩ϵ

= _____

Block Art

Shade in the square blocks in the empty grid on the right to match the design pattern given on the left in each case. You can make it colorful by using different colors too!

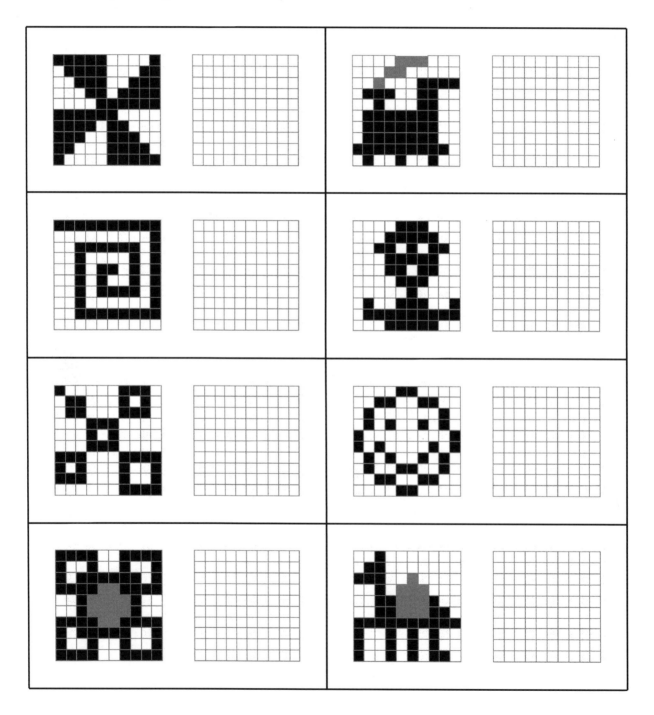

In each row, find the design that doesn't match the others (or find the odd one out)

1.

2.

3.

Hidden meaning

Each of these words and the way they are designed, make a popular phrase. Find what each one says.

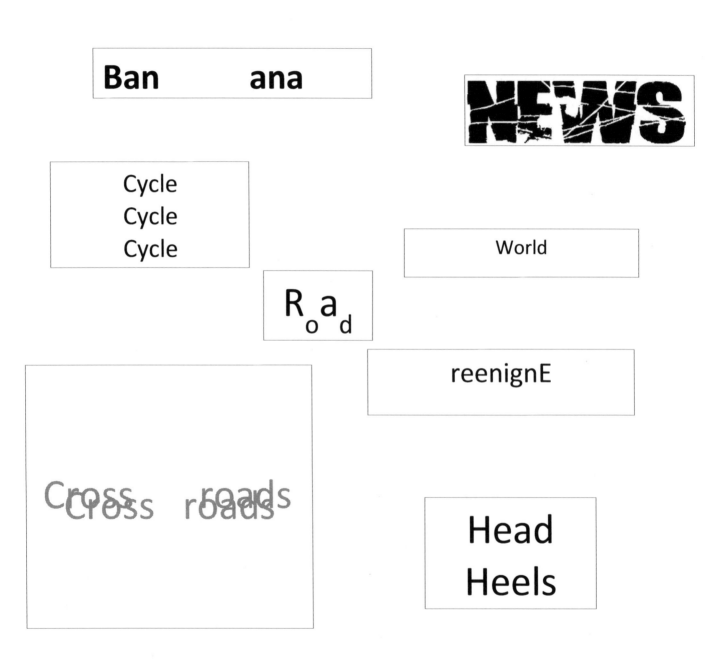

An artist has sent pictures for two stories. In both, a fisherman baits the hook, and casts it in the water, but in **Story 1**, a fish attracted by the bait, takes it and the fisherman gets his catch. In **Story 2**, the fish gets a brilliant idea and escapes by attaching a piece of broken net to the hook.

Can you put the picture in correct order for the two stories? Write the alphabets of the four pictures for each story in correct order. Some of the pictures could be common to both the stories.

Story 1   Story 2

-----, -----, -----, -----   -----, -----, -----, -----

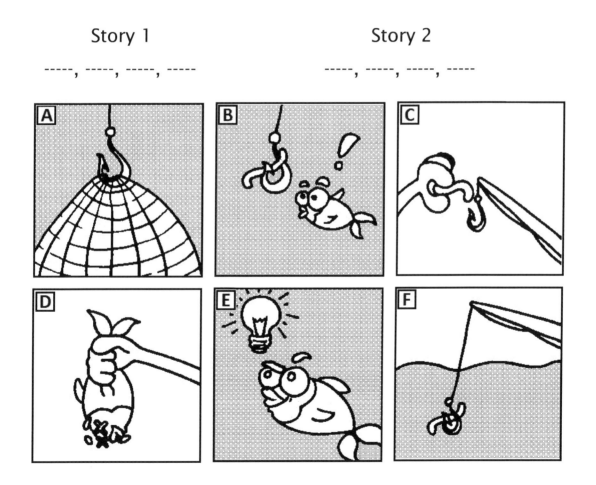

Answer Key

Find Patterns

While finding a pattern or a set of symbols, it is easier to look for a
single symbol that is easy to remember and locate. E.g. here, the
horse head (for the knight on the chess board) or the crown the
familiar shapes. Look for them. If they appear in multiple places,
check what is on the right/left or top/bottom. If that matches too,
check further. Otherwise move on to the next location where you
see it.

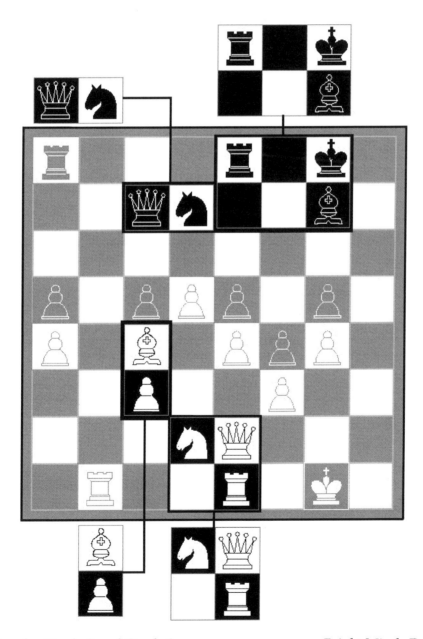

Vertical and Horizontal match

The word in the first row must have the first letter of all words!

EEL, ALE, PEA	TEN, ONE, GOT
P E A	G O T
E E L	O N E
A L E	T E N

TEA, HAT, ATE	GEM, BIG, ICE
H A T	B I G
A T E	I C E
T E A	G E M

CAR, ERA, ACE	EYE, LEG, GEL
A C E	G E L
C A R	E Y E
E R A	L E G

AREA, CART, REAP, TAPE	IDEA, DIME, MESS, EASY
C A R T	D I M E
A R E A	I D E A
R E A P	M E S S
T A P E	E A S Y

Pascal Triangle

Here the number in any circle is the sum of the two numbers above. So one must start from the topmost blank circle and work ones way downward, row by row.

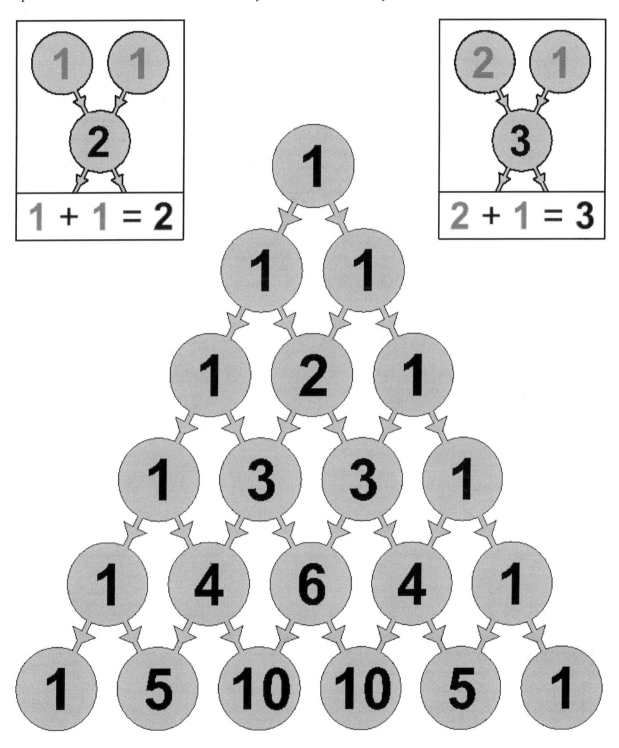

Mirror Image

Reflections of certain letters are readable simply by turning the book upside down. For example, the letters A, M, i etc. Others can then be read or guessed with context. After some practice, try reading without turning the book upside down. It helps sharpen the skill to visualize an object from a different point of view.

Math is fun!

Following are images of some words - what do the words say:

The frog starting from 1 and skipping every other stone would make it step on only the odd numbered stones: 1. 3. 5. 7. .... An odd number always ends with one of the following digits {1, 3, 5, 7, 9}, while even numbers stones – which the frog will skip – always end in one of the following digits {0, 2, 4, 6, 8}

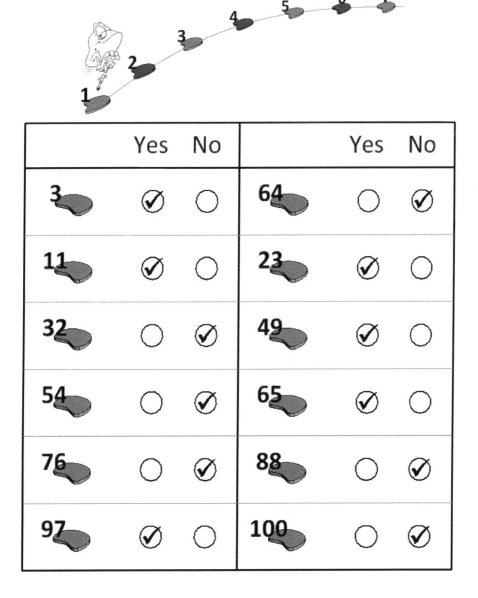

	Yes	No		Yes	No
3	✓	○	64	○	✓
11	✓	○	23	✓	○
32	○	✓	49	✓	○
54	○	✓	65	✓	○
76	○	✓	88	○	✓
97	✓	○	100	○	✓

Even and Odd #2

Even Steven the kangaroo likes to hop from one even number bush to the next. So it will land on bush numbers: 2, 4, 6, 8, 10 … An even number always ends with one of the following digits {2, 4, 6, 8, 0}

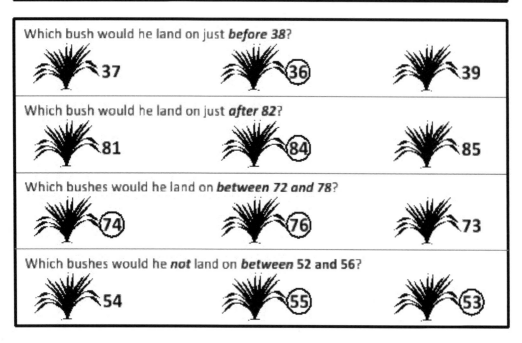

Connecting the odd numbers 1, 3, 5, 7, 9, 11 .... up to 71 reveals a **shoe**. While connecting the even numbers 2, 4, 6, 8, ... up to 92 reveals a **hat**.

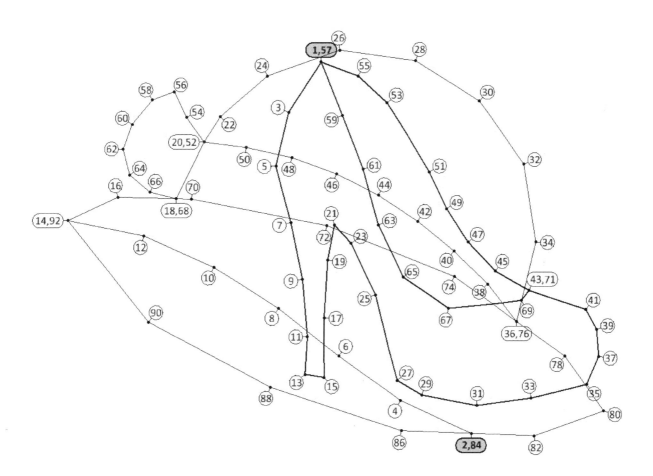

Connecting the odd numbers 1, 3, 5, 7, 9, 11 .... up to 101 reveals a **jet airplane**. While connecting the even numbers 2, 4, 6, 8, ... up to 102 reveals a **palm tree**.

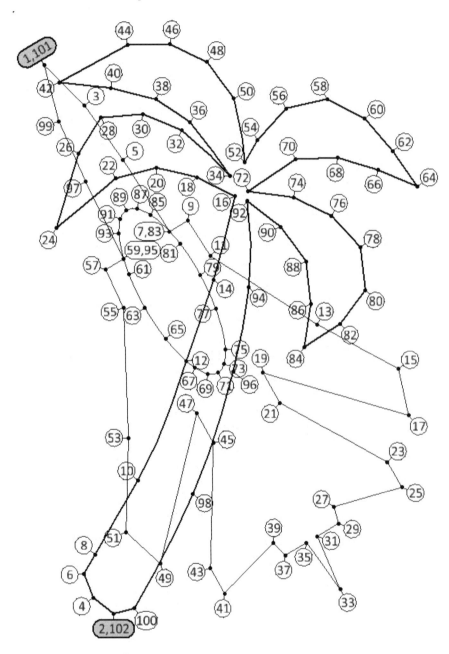

Skip Counting

To read the message, we need to rad the 5th, 10th, 15th, 20th letters. Did you notice all these numbers end with either a 0 or a 5? That makes counting by five very easy. Mark or highlight these letters now to reveal the secret message –

The King is arriving

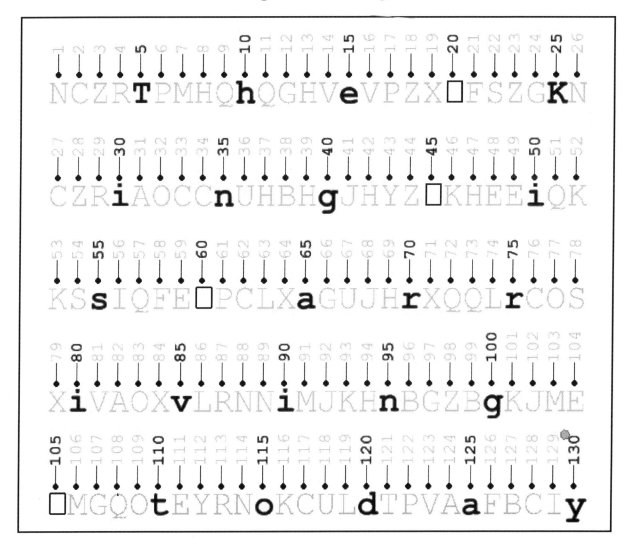

Hundreds, Tens and Ones

Here we have ones, tens and hundreds forming three digit numbers. Individual cube are counted as *ones*. The bars of ten are counted as the *tens* and the sheet of hundred are counted as the *hundreds*. So simply count and write the number of sheets in the hundreds place, number of bars in the tens place and the number of individual cubes in the unit or ones place to get the count.

Remember: if there are no bars, count them as **zero** bars and write a **zero** in the tens place. Similarly, if there are no individual cubes, count them as **zero** cubes and write a **zero** in the unit place.

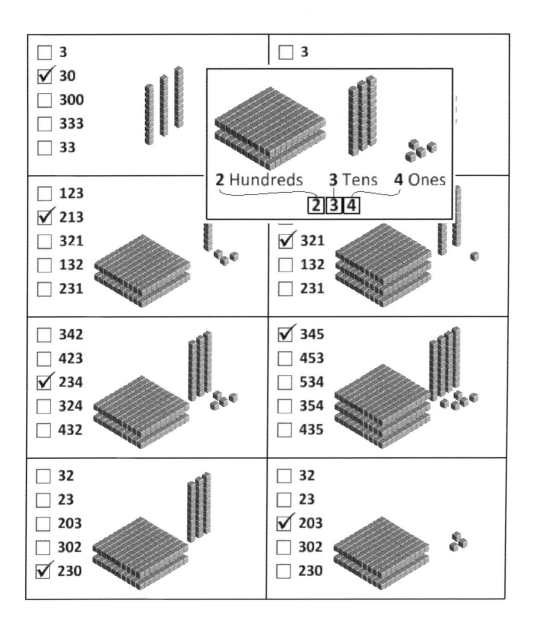

- [ ] 3
- [x] **30**
- [ ] 300
- [ ] 333
- [ ] 33

- [ ] 3

2 Hundreds   **3** Tens   **4** Ones

2 3 4

- [ ] 123
- [x] **213**
- [ ] 321
- [ ] 132
- [ ] 231

- [x] **321**
- [ ] 132
- [ ] 231

- [ ] 342
- [ ] 423
- [x] **234**
- [ ] 324
- [ ] 432

- [x] **345**
- [ ] 453
- [ ] 534
- [ ] 354
- [ ] 435

- [ ] 32
- [ ] 23
- [ ] 203
- [ ] 302
- [x] **230**

- [ ] 32
- [ ] 23
- [x] **203**
- [ ] 302
- [ ] 230

Place Values

The value of a digit changes with its place! In the tens place, it's multiplied by 10, in the hundreds place by 100 and so on. In the ones place, the value remains the same as it's multiplied by 1

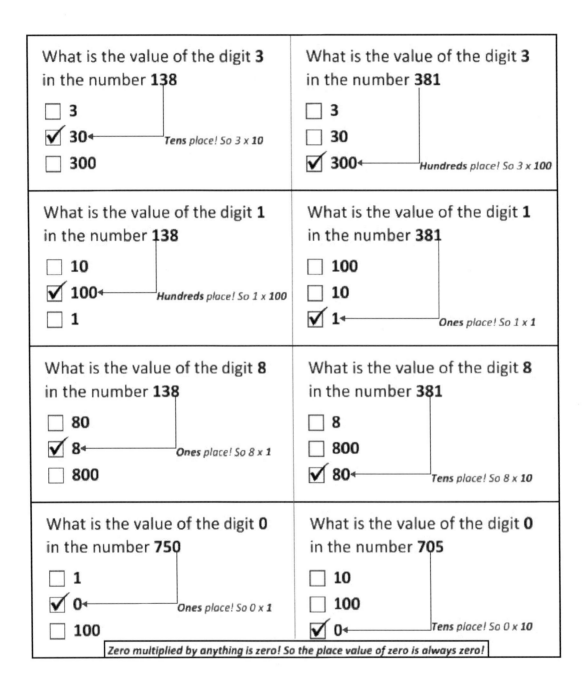

Find the Object

Grids use rows and columns to identify a location. Here the rows are given numbers, while the columns are given alphabets. E.g. to find the object at position (C3) Go down column (C) till you reach row number (3). Then mark the object there from the choices given.

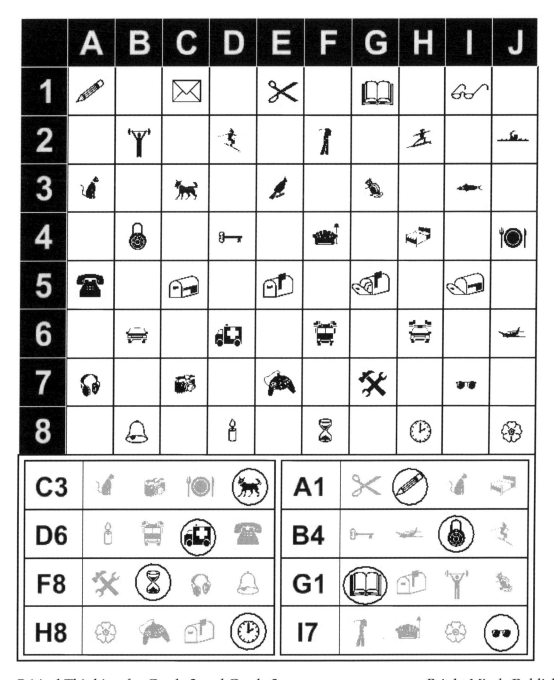

Cryptography

Cryptographs are lot easier to read if the alphabets are linked to the symbols (glyphs) with some mental image. Did you notice any such links? E.g. A is an Aeroplane, B is a Bell, X is similar to a scissor in shape ... You can guess the letters much faster this way and confirm from the given scheme of coding. Also, once you get most part of the word or the sentence, the rest can be guessed, which makes it easier to look up the code.

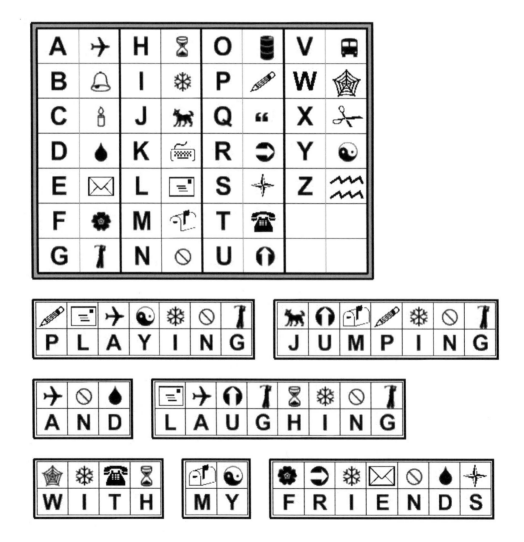

General strategy: Here we have three horizontal Rows numbered 1, 2, 3 and five vertical columns labeled A, B, C, D, E. Each of these has one or more missing numbers. *It is impossible to solve the row or a column, when there is more than one missing number.* So we must start with those with only a single missing number, keeping in mind that that the quantities on the right and left of an equal to sign must be equal. Find one side and then figure the number missing on the other side.

For example,

$$2 + 3 + 1 = \_\_\_ + 4$$

Here, on the left of the equal to sign adds up to 6.

So, the right side must amount to 6 too, of which we already have 4.

So, the missing number must be 2!

Solving all the rows and columns with a single missing number, makes some of the other rows and columns solvable! So we take them up next and so on ...

COLUMN A : 1 + 2 = **3**

COLUMN B : 2 + 4 = 6

COLUMN C : 3 - 1 = **2**

Columns D and E cannot be solved at this stage, because they have more than one missing numbers. So, let us work on the rows next.

ROW 1   : 1 + 2 + 3 = **1** + 5

ROW 2   : 2 + 4 - 1 = 3 + **2**

Row 3 still has two unknows. So solve column D

COLUMN D : 1 + 3 = **4**

ROW 3   : 3 + 6 + 2 = 4 + **7**

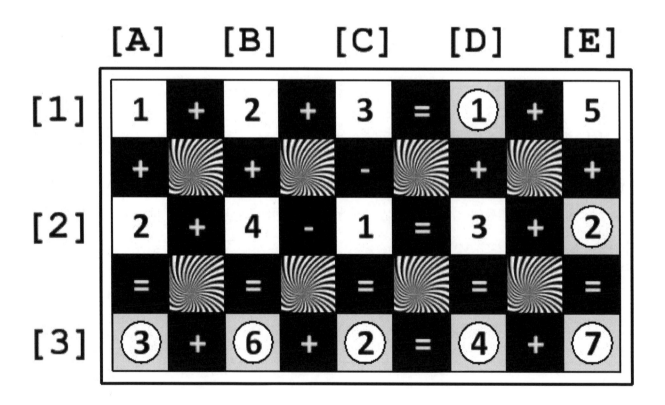

Number Quilt #2

COLUMN A : $1 + 2 = 3$

COLUMN B : $2 + 4 = 6$

COLUMN C : $3 - 1 = 2$

Columns D and E are impossible at this stage, but rows 1 and 2 have become solvable!

ROW 1 : $1 + 2 + 3 = 1 + 5$

ROW 2 : $2 + 4 - 1 = 3 + 2$

Now we can solve columns D and E!

COLUMN D : $1 + 3 = 3$

COLUMN E : $5 + 2 = 7$

Did you notice this quilt is identical to the previous one? Only the missing patches were different.

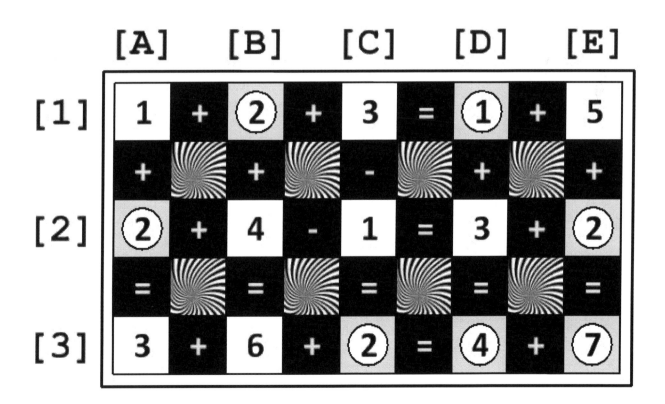

Number Quilt #3

COLUMN A : 5 + 10 = **15**

COLUMN B : 10 + 20 = **30**

COLUMN C : 15 + 5 = **10**

Columns D and E are impossible at this stage, but rows 1 and 2 are solvable

ROW 1   : 5 + 10 + 15 = **5** + 25

ROW 2   : 10 + 20 - 5 = 15 + **10**

Columns D and E are now solvable!

COLUMN D : 5 + 15 = **20**

COLUMN E : 25 + 10 = **35**

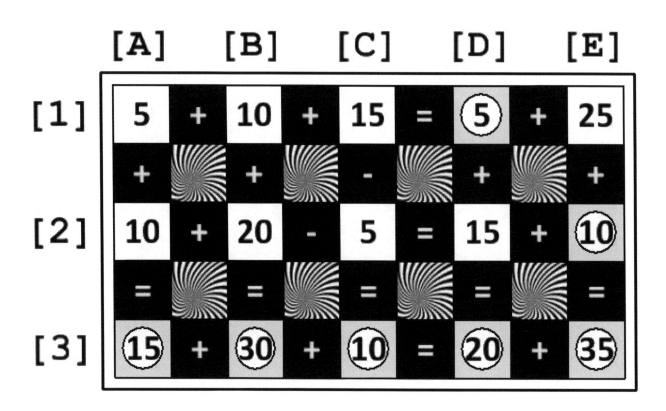

Number Quilt #4

Rows 1, 2, 3 and columns D and E contain more than one missing number, so it is impossible to solve them for now. So let us start with columns A, B and C

COLUMN A : $3 + 6 = 9$

COLUMN B : $6 + 12 = 18$

COLUMN C : $9 - 3 = 6$

Columns D and E are impossible at this stage, but rows 1 and 2 are solvable

ROW 1 : $3 + 6 + 9 = 3 + 15$

ROW 2 : $6 + 12 - 3 = 9 + 6$

Columns D and E are now solvable!

COLUMN D : $3 + 9 = 12$

COLUMN E : $15 + 6 = 21$

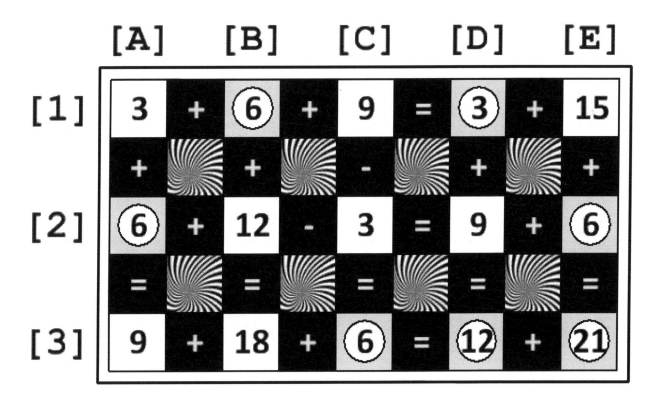

Number Quilt #5

Rows 1, 2, 3 and columns A and D contain more than one missing number. So it is impossible to solve them for now. So let us start with columns B, C, E

COLUMN B :   3 + 7 = 10

COLUMN C :   8 * 4 = 4

COLUMN E :   6 - 2 = 4

Rows 1 and 2 are solvable

ROW 1   :   1 + 3 + 8 = 18 + 6

ROW 2   :   5 + 7 = 4 + 6 + 2

Columns A and D are now solvable!

COLUMN A :   1 + 5 = 6

COLUMN D :   18 + 6 = 24

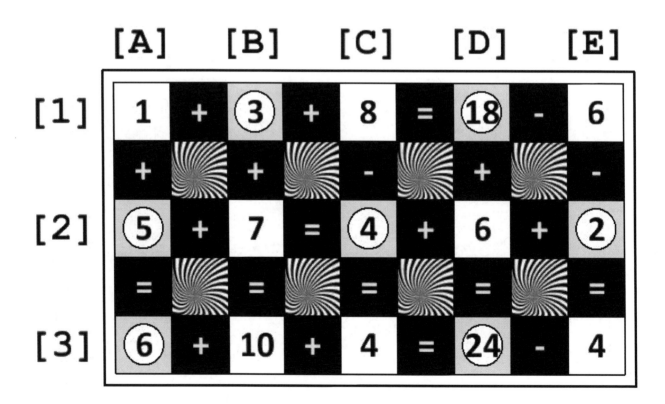

Strategy: To check, imagine the letter or alphabet being folded on to itself. Would the two parts fit exactly on top of each other? Then the fold-line itself is the life of symmetry! Some letters and alphabets, have even two of those!

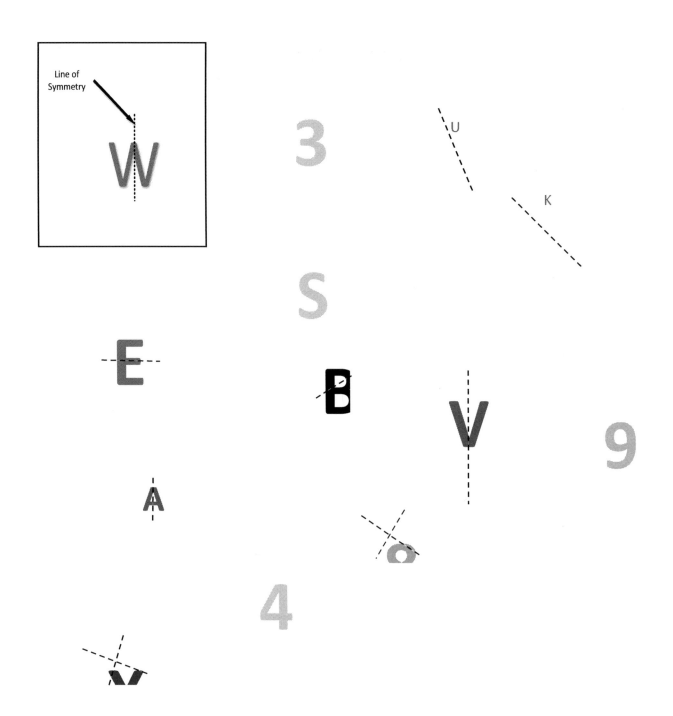

Line of
Symmetry

W

3

U

K

S

E

B

V

9

A

4

Garbled Proverb

Hint: The proverb starts with a word starting with a capital letter!

Make sure the proverb uses all the words given.

[1] ends that All's well well

Proverb: All's well that ends well

[2] makes perfect Practice.

Proverb: Practice makes perfect

[3] sure race Slow but the wins.

Proverb: Slow but sure wins the race

[4] the is policy best Honesty

Proverb: Honesty is the best policy

[5] while the shines hay Make sun.

Proverb: Make hay while the sun shines

[6] before you Look leap

Proverb: Look before you leap

[7] indeed A friend friend is a need in

Proverb: A friend in need is a friends indeed

[8] the spice is Variety of life

Proverb: Variety is a spice of life

[9] bird catches worm early The the

Proverb: The early bird catches the worm

[10] Birds feather together of a flock

Proverb: Birds of feather flock together

In this exercise, some order of counting the squares ensures that no squares are missed. For example, one can start from the smallest squares (let's call them 1 × 1) numbered 1, 2, 3, ... Then the bigger squares (2 × 2) marked as groups of (1, 2, 4, 5), (2, 3, 5, 6) etc. Finally, the largest outermost (3 × 3) square that enclosed everything should be counted.

Count Squares 01   9 + 4 + 1= 14 squares

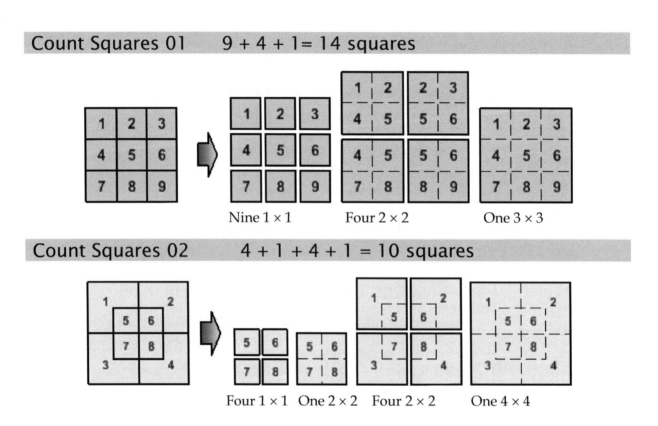

Nine 1 × 1   Four 2 × 2   One 3 × 3

Count Squares 02   4 + 1 + 4 + 1 = 10 squares

Four 1 × 1   One 2 × 2   Four 2 × 2   One 4 × 4

Counting Triangles

In this exercise, some order of counting the triangles ensures that no triangles are missed. For example, one can start from the smallest triangles numbered 1, 2, 3,.... Then the bigger triangles made of four smaller triangles.

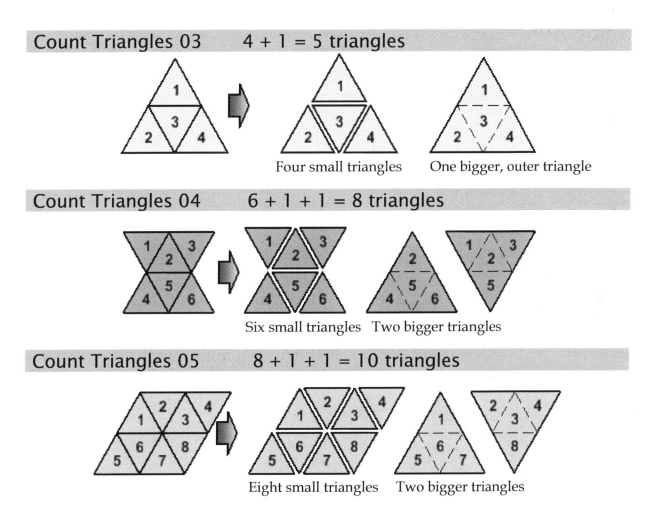

Count Triangles 03   4 + 1 = 5 triangles

Four small triangles   One bigger, outer triangle

Count Triangles 04   6 + 1 + 1 = 8 triangles

Six small triangles   Two bigger triangles

Count Triangles 05   8 + 1 + 1 = 10 triangles

Eight small triangles   Two bigger triangles

Palindromes

Palindromes are words that read the same way from both directions (example: Mom). So they must begin and end with the same alphabet! This clue itself will help you eliminate many words that are not palindromes. For others you can try reading them backward letter by letter. Getting the same words back? It's a palindrome then!

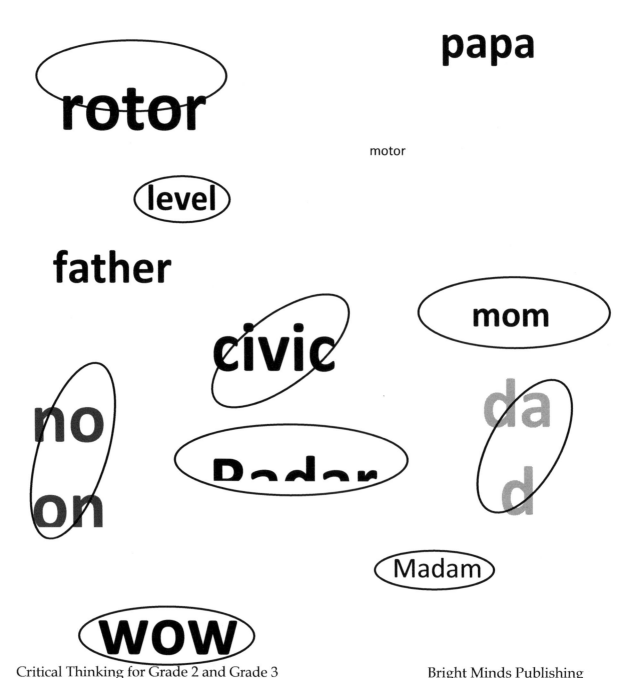

papa

rotor

motor

level

father

civic

mom

no on

Radar

dad

Madam

WOW

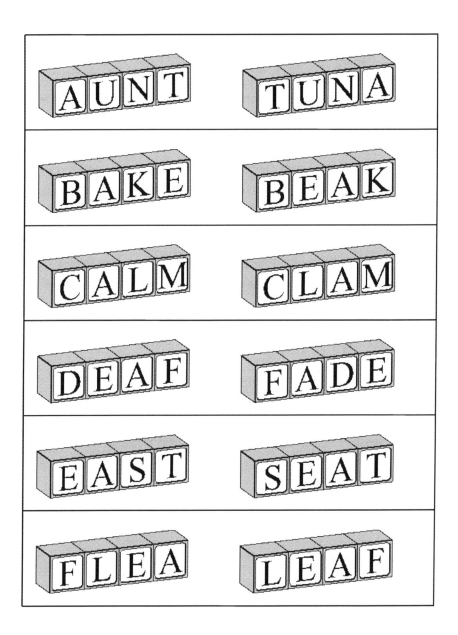

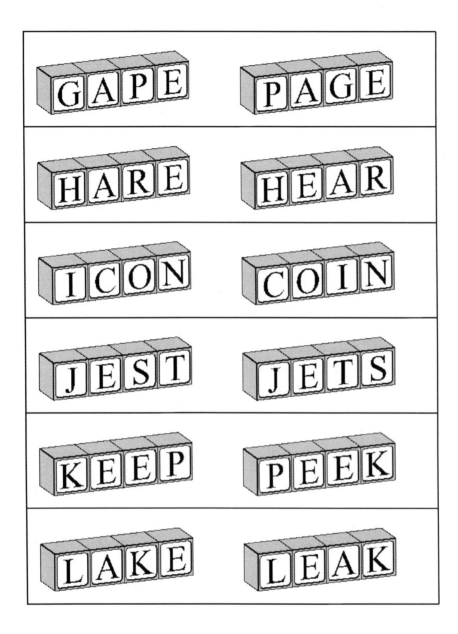

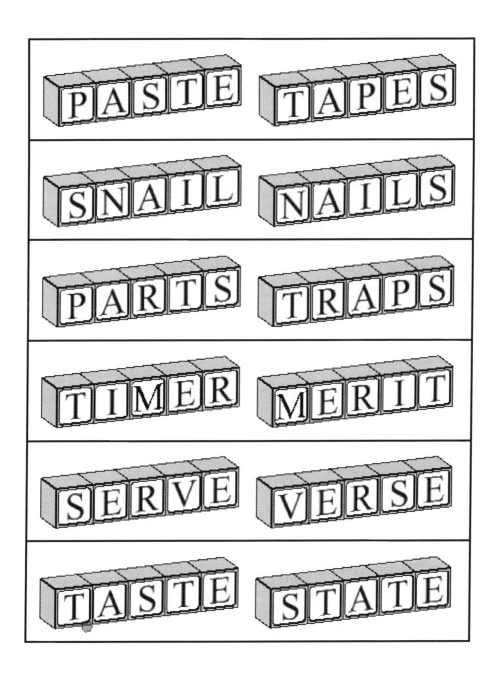

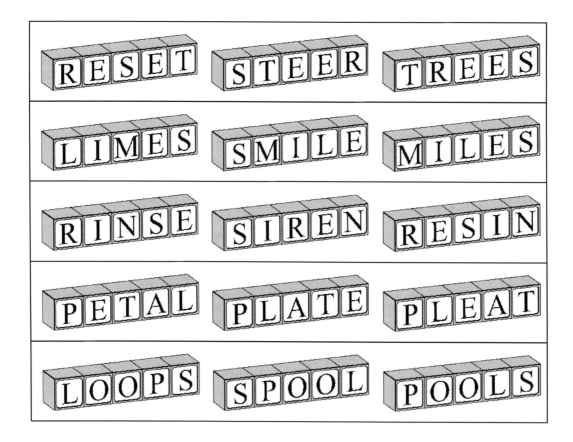

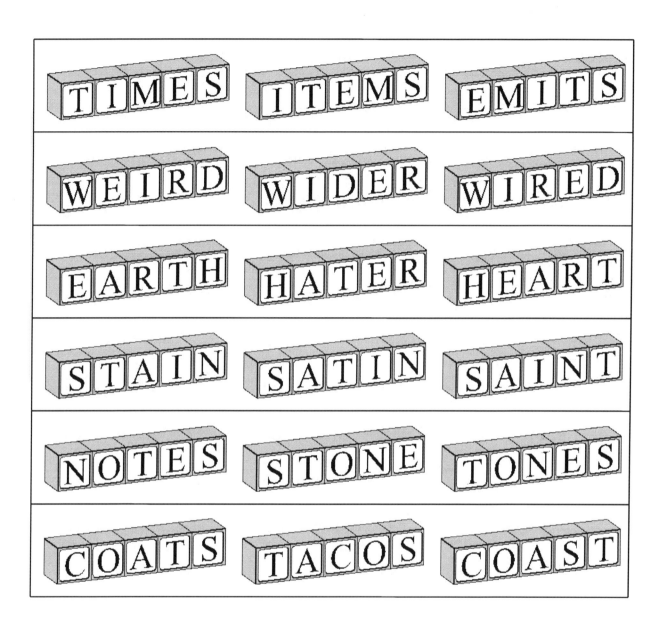

Maze Puzzles

Mazes Strategy	**Square Maze**
The most confusing part of a maze is the branching - multiple ways we can take from some points. But if we take them one by one in some order and mark the one that lead to dead ends, any maze can be solved without wasting time in repetition. Work with a pencil and an eraser and cross out that paths that lead nowhere. If none of the branches work, go back to the previous point of branching and try.	

Pentagonal Maze	**Hexagonal Maze**

Hexagonal Hive Maze	**Storm Clouds Maze**

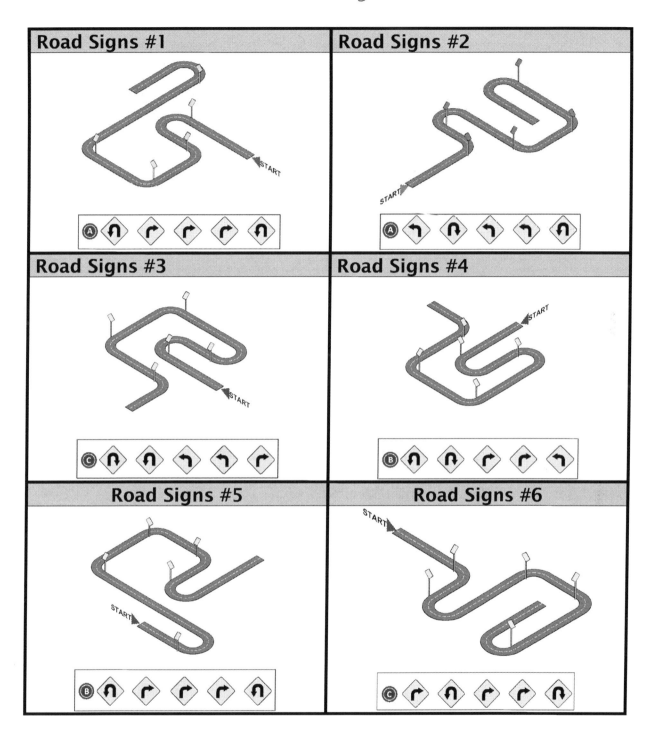

Strategy: In this set of exercises, splitting the given stack of solids into smaller subgroups makes the counting easier. Two possible ways of such subgrouping is shown below -

Layers: The subgroups could be layers L1, L2, L3 as shown. Count the solids in each layer and add them. Layers could be horizontal too.

Columns: Imagine the given heap of solids as if made of columns. Any solid whose top face can be seen is at the top of such a column or a tower. Estimate the height of each tower and add them up.

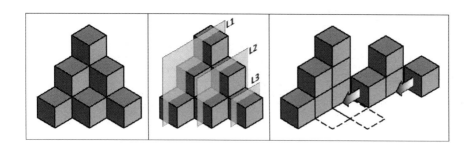
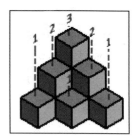

Layers   **Columns**

S1 Count the cubes

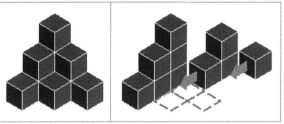

$$10 = 6 + 3 + 1$$

S2 Count the Cylinders

$$12 = 2 + 5 + 5$$

Count the mugs

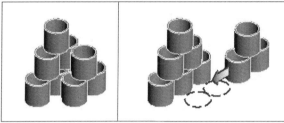

$$9 = 6 + 3$$

Count the Hexagonal Prisms

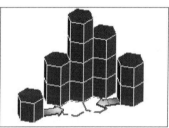

$$12 = 9 + 1 + 2$$

Count the Pentagonal Prisms

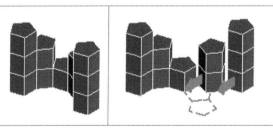

$$11 = 6 + 2 + 3$$

Count the Triangular Prisms

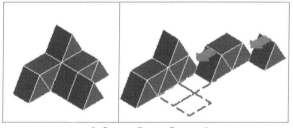

$$10 = 6 + 3 + 1$$

This exercise involves both addition and subtraction.

If the top block and one of the supporting blocks are given, then, subtract the value of the bottom block from the top to get the value of the other supporting block.

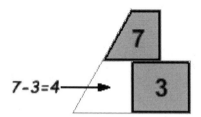

If the two supporting blocks are given, just add them to get the top one.

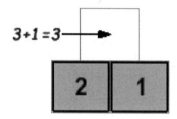

And be sure to check the shape of the block needed! A boat may carry the block with the correct numbers, but they may not have the correct shape to occupy fit in the empty place in the pyramid.

Number Pyramid #1

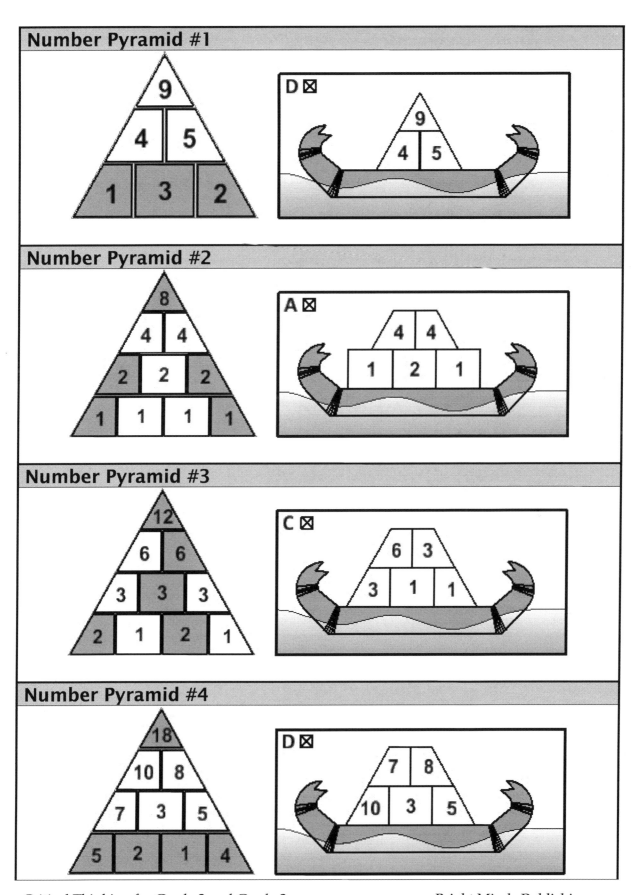

Number Pyramid #1

9

4 5

1 3 2

D ☒

9

4 5

Number Pyramid #2

8

4 4

2 2 2

1 1 1 1

A ☒

4 4

1 2 1

Number Pyramid #3

12

6 6

3 3 3

2 1 2 1

C ☒

6 3

3 1 1

Number Pyramid #4

18

10 8

7 3 5

5 2 1 4

D ☒

7 8

10 3 5

Number Pyramid #5

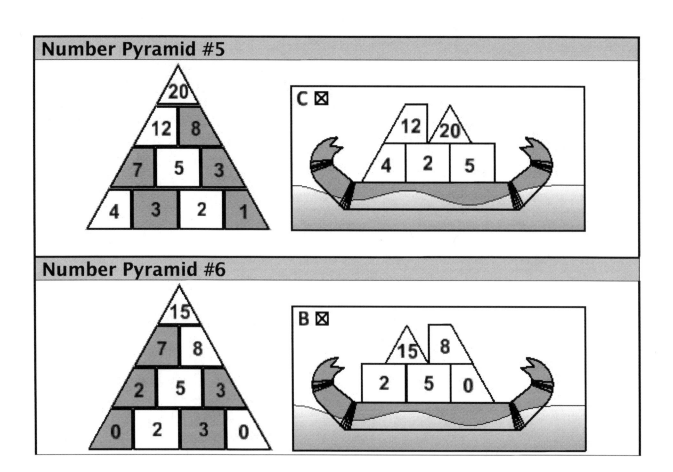

Number Pyramid #6

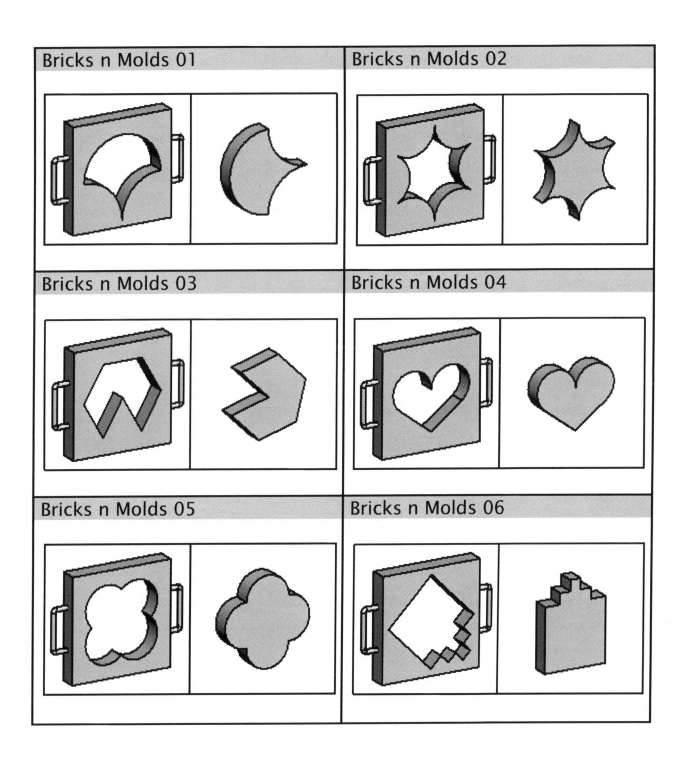

Bricks n Molds 01

Bricks n Molds 02

Bricks n Molds 03

Bricks n Molds 04

Bricks n Molds 05

Bricks n Molds 06

Coins 01

1	✓	1
2	✓	2
4	✓	4
8	☐	0
16	☐	0

7

Coins 02

1	✓	1
2	✓	2
4	☐	0
8	✓	8
16	☐	0

11

Coins 03

1	✓	1
2	✓	2
4	☐	0
8	☐	0
16	✓	16

19

Coins 04

1	✓	1
2	✓	2
4	✓	4
8	☐	0
16	✓	16

23

Coins 05

1	☐	0
2	✓	2
4	☐	0
8	✓	8
16	✓	16

26

Coins 06

1	☐	0
2	✓	2
4	✓	4
8	✓	8
16	✓	16

30

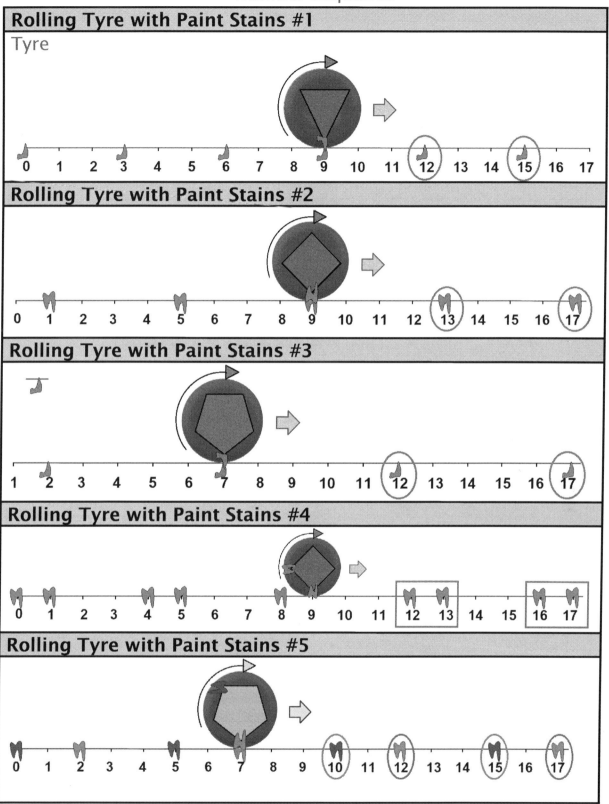

Rolling Tyre with Paint Stains #1

Tyre

Rolling Tyre with Paint Stains #2

Rolling Tyre with Paint Stains #3

Rolling Tyre with Paint Stains #4

Rolling Tyre with Paint Stains #5

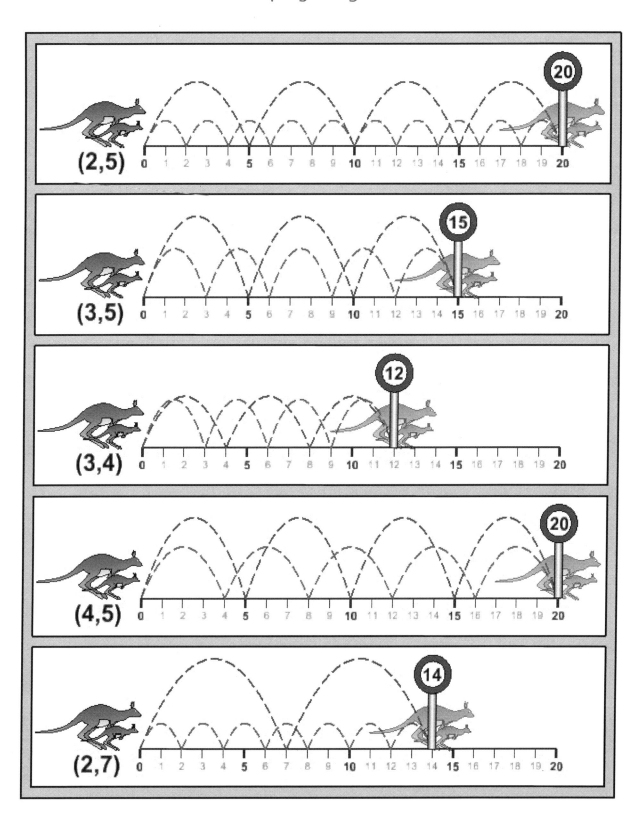

Here, look up each symbol in the given table and replace it with the symbol it is paired to.

A = ꝺ	B = ℧	C = Ⅎ	D = ꞌΩ
Ɛ = Γ	F = Δ	G = Π	H = Σ
I = Φ	J = Ƅ	K = ɸ	L = ϵ
M = ʔ	N = ₵	O = Ω	P = Ɜ
Q = Ж	R = Φ̄	S = △	T = ⊥̇
U = ∩	V = ∉	W = ∏	X = Σ
Y = ζ	Z = ⊼		

The message "*I love my family*" can be encoded as shown below

I		L	O	V	E		M	Y		F	A	M	I	L	Y
Φ		ϵ	Ω	∉	Γ		ʔ	ζ		Δ	ꝺ	ʔ	Φ	ϵ	ζ

Use the same method to break the code:

"Σꝺ Πꝺ Φ Φ   Φ△ ℧ Γ ꝺ∩⊥̇ Φ Δ ∩ϵ"

Σ	ꝺ	Π	ꝺ	Φ	Φ		Φ	△		℧	Γ	ꝺ	∩	⊥̇	Φ	Δ	∩	ϵ
H	A	W	A	I	I		I	S		B	E	A	U	T	I	F	U	L

Block Art

Strategy: For a precise replication of the pattern, you may number or mark the rows and columns in some way. This helps identifying a square and tell you where you are if you feel lost in the grid!

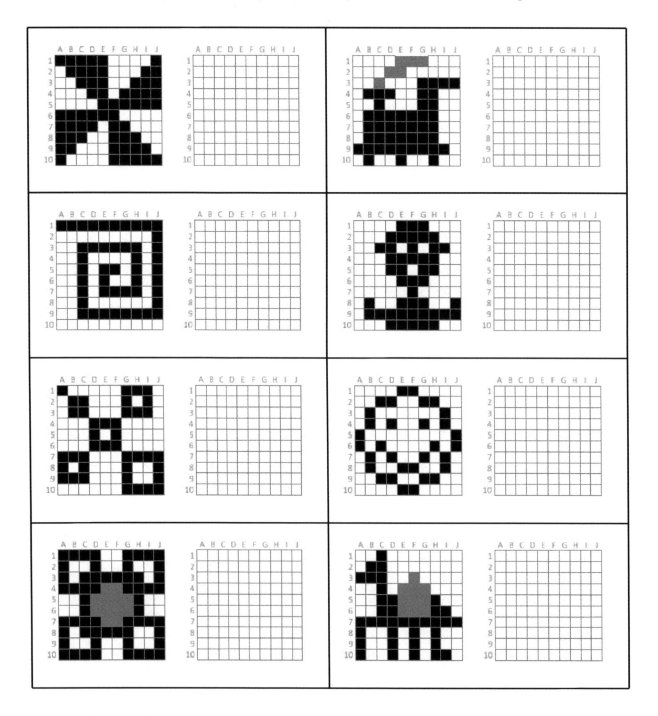

To find the design that doesn't match the others, select any part of a pattern – say the outermost ring or the innermost core – and compare it with the others. If it matches, select another part and so on, until a mismatch is found.

1.

2.

3.

Hidden Meaning

Strategy: Combine the visual and verbal clues to form a phrase.

Ban ana	Here, the word **Banana** is **split** into two parts thus **Banana Split**!

Here, the word **NEWS** is all cracked and **broken** giving us some **Breaking News**!

Cycle Cycle Cycle	Here, the word **Cycle** is repeated **thrice** thus building a **Tricycle**!

World	Here, the word **World** occupies a small part of a large rectangle, suggesting it is a **Small world**!

R_oa_d	Here, the letters of the word **Road** have gone up and down, like a **Bumpy Road** or a **Bumpy Ride**!

Here word **Crossroads** is crossing itself, forming **Crossroads**!

Cross roads
Cross roads

Reenigne

Head Heels

Stories with Pictures

Both the stories have the fisherman bait the hook (**C**), and casts it in the water (**F**), so both will begin with the same two pictures.

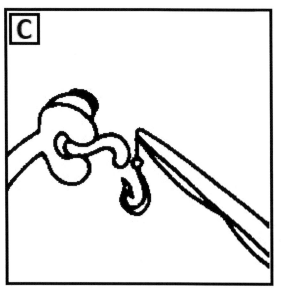

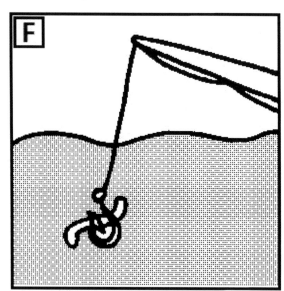

Next in **Story 1**, a fish attracted by the bait (**B**), takes it and the fisherman gets his catch (**D**).

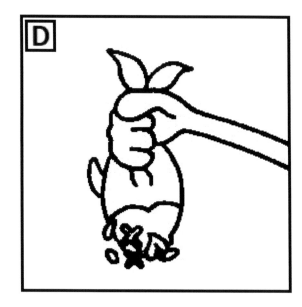

But in **Story 2**, the fish gets a brilliant idea (**E**) and escapes by attaching a piece of broken net to the hook (**A**).

 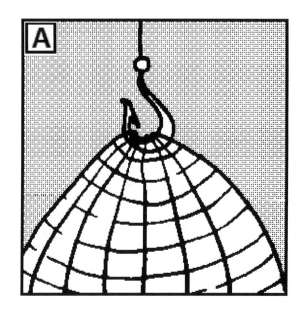

So, the picture sequences for the two stories are -

Story 1: **C, F, B, D**

Story 2: **C, F, E, A**

Made in the USA
Las Vegas, NV
09 April 2021

21144783R00081